LORD, I WISH MY FAMILY WOULD GET SAVED

LARRY KEEFAUVER, D. MIN.

CREATION HOUSE

LORD, I WISH MY FAMILY WOULD GET SAVED
by Larry Keefauver, D.Min.
Published by Creation House
A division of Strang Communications Company
600 Rinehart Road
Lake Mary, Florida 32746
www.creationhouse.com

Library of Congress Catalog Card Number: 99-98132
International Standard Book Number: 0-88419-678-X

The names and details regarding individuals in this book have been changed (with the exception of my family members). Any similarities to actual persons or incidents is purely coincidental.

0 1 2 3 4 5 VP 8 7 6 5 4 3 2

Printed in the United States of America

To the Lord Jesus Christ,
Whose shed blood has saved me and my household.
To Jesus be honor, glory and praise forever.

AMEN

To my wife, Judi, whose prayers, support and love have sustained me.

We rejoice in the salvation of our children (Amy, Peter and Patrick) and their families.

We continue to pray for the salvation of our children's children, our relatives and all our family members.

I express my deepest gratitude to...

My wife, Judi, who loves me and believes in my gift-ings.

My children and grandchildren, who are the joy of my life—Amy, Lee, Judah, Asher, Peter, Patrick and Elizabeth.

My parents, Jim and Sara, who shared Jesus with me.

Tom and Cathy Laws, my family who encourages me.

My Sunday school teachers, pastors and youth leaders at First Christian Church in Ft. Lauderdale, Florida, who nurtured me in the faith.

My in-laws, Terry and Doris, who prayed for us.

Stephen and Joy Strang for their prayers and support in my writing.

Dave Welday, Rick Nash, Barbara Dycus and all the Creation House editors and staff, who are so gracious and kind in assisting me.

Pastor Sam Hinn and the pastors, elders and deacons of The Gathering Place Worship Center in Lake Mary, Florida, who pray for me.

Paul Little, whose influence in evangelism through IVCF impacted my life.

All the prayer support partners of YMCS, whose prayers have now undergirded my family for over a decade.

CONTENTS

SECTION IV:
FORTY DAYS OF PRAYER: GETTING YOUR FAMILY SAVED . . 187

INTRODUCTION

WHO IS LOST IN
YOUR HOUSE?

⁀

My wife, Judi, and I have had the privilege of praying with thousands of families around the nation during our prayer seminars, and we have prayed with many of them for the salvation of their lost loved ones. During these times of prayer, we have listened to their personal stories— their attempts to share the Good News, their frustration, sadness, guilt and even anger.

. I know your heart aches for your lost family members. Maybe you tried to tell them about Jesus, but you were met with polite disinterest, rebuttals or even fierce anger. I've discovered that most Christians experience this because they care so much about their loved ones. And I've also discovered that many of the stories are the same.

Let me share a few with you.

Scott...lost at college

Scott had been raised in church. In fact, at summer camp during his junior year he heard God's voice call him into ministry. He went to college a solid Christian, but by his second or third visit home, his parents realized that he was changing. Seeds of doubt had been sown into his heart by a professor who taught an introductory philosophy course. And those seeds had produced cynicism that was growing into outright rebellion.

Scott's parents were worried and guilt ridden. They blamed themselves for allowing Scott to attend a state university with all of his friends instead of the Bible college recommended by their pastor. They had felt that Scott was strong in faith and well grounded enough to hold his own in the university atmosphere. Now it seemed they had been wrong.

Scott talked to them about the different philosophies he was being taught. He was impressed by the intellectual prowess of his professor and the new ways of looking at the world he was learning. Scott didn't attempt to find a solid support group of Christian friends, even among the many Christian campus organizations. Instead of worshiping on Sundays, he slept in after a long Saturday night of partying. Isolated from the body of Christ, Scott began doubting. He quit praying and became skeptical about his faith.

Jack...good husband and dad with no need for God

While Jennifer dated Jack he was very interested in going to church with her. They had long discussions about her faith and the Bible. At every altar call, Jennifer just knew this would be the time Jack would go forward and accept Christ.

Jack's conversion never happened, but Jennifer was so in love with him that she moved ahead with the wedding plans. *With God, nothing is impossible,* she thought. She believed God would "work on" Jack, and soon after the wedding he would be saved.

The big day came, and then the honeymoon. Then they settled into a routine. Weeks became months, and months stretched into years. Jack remained curious and interested in spiritual things, never interfering with Jennifer's going to church or actively pursuing God. Jennifer prayed continually for Jack to be saved, but she finally grew frustrated that he was so close yet so far from becoming a Christian.

Jennifer couldn't complain about his behavior. Jack was a good and loving husband and father. He worked hard, provided everything the family needed and enjoyed life. He simply never saw the need for what he called "religious emotionalism." To him, going to church was for women and children, but not for real men. Christianity to Jack was being a good person, which he tried hard to be.

Jack never crossed over from trying to be good to the imparted righteousness that comes only from knowing Jesus.

Veronica…a teen in rebellion

Throughout elementary school, Veronica lived the charmed life of a good student who was popular and well-behaved. She loved going to church, especially after truly receiving Christ one Sunday morning in Kid's Church. She loved life, and it showed. Everyone enjoyed being with her. Then adolescence hit hard.

Veronica stopped listening to her parents and started running with the wrong crowd at middle school. Her angry, "drop dead" looks took her parents by surprise. Everything she did and said dripped with scorn, and she rejected all that was traditional or spiritual. Authority figures—her parents, teachers, youth pastor, aunts, uncles and neighbors—all became the enemies.

Bewildered, her parents tried everything to get their sweet girl back—first grounding, then home schooling, then Christian school, then even tough love. Nothing worked. Veronica was bent on doing everything her way, even if it meant destroying herself. She clothed herself in black, shaved parts of her head, had her body pierced and listened to dark, destructive music. Finally, she ran away to the streets and disappeared into the shadows.

Her parents were in a state of shock, devastated and heartbroken. They had almost lost all hope that she would ever be restored to them or to Christ.

Agnes…a mom out of touch

Barbara and her mom, Agnes, hadn't communicated well for years. They had a good relationship when Barbara was young, but when she hit middle school and high school and began forming her own opinions, their relationship grew cool. Even through college, then during Barbara's job at a new software company, the coolness remained in their relationship.

Barbara and her mom had their moments of sharing and even tenderness, but they were rare. Agnes was unresponsive and seemed uncaring. She wasn't interested in what interested Barbara, and she made no attempt to act as if she were. She had her own friends in the clubs she belonged to, and they consumed her life.

Agnes had gone to church for years. She was religious, traditional, set in her beliefs and loyal to her church. She worked tirelessly at the yearly church bazaar and cooked occasionally at other church events.

Then Barbara experienced a life-changing encounter with Jesus through a friend at work, and she couldn't wait to tell her mom. However, Agnes rebuffed all of Barbara's attempts to share Christ with her, feeling that Barbara was arrogant in thinking that she needed "a personal relationship with Christ." After all, she had been going to church for years, and she dismissed Barbara's fervor as the passion of youth. Then she told Barbara in an unusually angry outburst never to bring up the subject again.

So Barbara reluctantly avoided talking with her mom about salvation. As her passionate love for Jesus grew, so did her grief at her mother's lack of interest.

Barbara knew that religion never saved anyone. Icy silence surrounded any possible reference to faith when mother and daughter communicated. Unless a thaw occurred, a mother could be lost for eternity.

Terry…a brother unreachable

For Terry, mysticism and the New Age beliefs answered his need for spirituality. He practiced yoga and meditated for half an hour each morning. That brought him peace and centered him. He sought out people who were loving, and he freely gave of his possessions to the needy.

Terry's sister, Monica, had recently met Jesus, and she was eager to share her newfound faith with him. He listened attentively, and he was very tolerant and accepting. In fact, he told Monica that Jesus was indeed a great prophet, and he encouraged Monica to continue seeking for the wisdom of the ages that the Christ represented.

From then on, every time Monica shared a scripture or tried to witness to her brother, a polite wall arose between them. Terry didn't want to offend his sister, and he liked to avoid the tension of arguments at all costs. So he agreed with her on every point except her narrow-minded view that everyone who didn't "accept Jesus" would go to hell. Terry didn't believe a loving God would create hell, and his gentle arguments often overwhelmed and confused Monica.

Monica felt inadequate, and she always left Terry's presence feeling a little bewildered about her own beliefs. Yet she knew beyond a doubt that Jesus was her Lord and her Savior, and she desperately wanted Terry to know Him as well.

Do You Have a Lost Family Member?

Did one of these stories ring true for you? Perhaps you recognized yourself or one of your family members. Maybe you feel hopeless, desperate and confused about what to do next. Or perhaps you've gone from hopelessness to anger, then paralyzing frustration. Maybe you're just sad, worried and fearful, and that has you unable to make the next move.

Perhaps all your unsuccessful attempts to share Christ have led you to believe that your loved one is unreachable. If you feel that way, you're wrong. No one is ever beyond the reach of the long arm of God's loving mercy and compassion.

You may be impatient, but God is eternally patient. You may be angry, but God is unconditional love. You may be out of words to express your faith, but God's Spirit always has a fresh word and new way to touch the lost.

You may believe it's too late, but the God of the second chance declares that it's never too late. Your faith may be exhausted, your determination expended and your love tested to the maximum, but God's love is endless. His determination is eternal, and He doesn't run out of hope.

I want you to know that you can receive a new infusion of hope, determination and even joy concerning the salvation of your loved ones. Perhaps all you need is a fresh way of looking at the situation and a new way of loving your family and reaching out to them with Christ's love. I believe that by the time you finish this book, you will have that.

But getting there will take a little courage, because we are going to look for any walls in us that are keeping our families from being saved. Yes, I said *in us*. Then we will look at any walls in our loved ones that are keeping them from Jesus and find out how we can lovingly break down those walls. We will learn how to reach beyond and over and around each other's walls so we can see our loved ones reconciled to Jesus.

If it takes a lifetime to reach your family members for Jesus, will you wait, pray, persist, love, share and give? A lifetime isn't too long to see all your family saved, but eternity is too long for any of them to be lost!

SECTION I

WHAT'S IN ME
THAT KEEPS THEM
FROM JESUS?

⤸

For years Sally tried to share Jesus with her brother, Joe, and his family. They lived in another state, so she sent them Christian books and tapes. When she visited them, she talked about Jesus often, hoping they would see the light. She genuinely wanted them to experience the joy she had in Christ.

But Sally also had a sharp tongue. She criticized everyone from the president to her pastor to the neighbor next door. And she did it around everyone—including her brother and his wife. In fact, it led them to wonder what she said about them when they weren't around.

Sally's critical and judgmental nature caused everyone around her to tread lightly so they wouldn't offend her and be subjected to scathing recriminations both in person and behind their backs. Because of that, the love of the Father simply didn't shine through Sally's life. Little wonder that Joe and his wife didn't want to know the Jesus she so brashly proclaimed.

Flaws are easy to spot in others but hard to see in ourselves. Yet most of us have flaws that become walls between us and our family members—and they can keep our loved ones from accepting the Good News of Christ.

Our unsaved family members are experts at spotting facades and masks! If we don't have a vital, personal relationship with Jesus, we won't succeed in passing the Good News on to those who need it. The Good News is that Jesus has saved us from sin and delivered us from darkness into light. However, we need to be living the gospel in order to share it. After all, our lives are the loudest witness we have.

Sharing Jesus with family members begins with us, not them.

THE WALLS IN US THAT KEEP OUR FAMILIES FROM JESUS

Every one of us has flaws. Some are little, and some are gigantic. The flaws in us that are large enough to make others stumble are often strongholds. What is a stronghold? In this case, let's think of it as a wall that blocks the light of Jesus from shining through us. That particular area of our heart is dark, and the devil rules in darkness.

Walls separate us from both our Lord and our families. For instance, in our physical bodies we are tempted by our lusts. In our souls, we are tempted in our thoughts (mind), feelings (affections) and decisions (will). When we continually or habitually sin in an area of our bodies or our souls, then we are building walls that can become strongholds in our lives.

A stronghold is constructed of the bricks of unconfessed sin in an area of our lives. For example, we may hold anger toward someone for a wrong done to us. As we let that anger foment in us, we add brick after brick to the wall of the stronghold. First, we are angry at the person who hurt us. We nurse and rehearse the hurt. One brick, two bricks. Our anger causes us to view the actions of others as intending to hurt us. Three bricks, four bricks, ten bricks. Eventually, we become angry at people in general because "they are all out to get us." Twenty bricks, fifty bricks, a whole wall.

The wall of a stronghold prevents the light of God's truth from entering that part of our lives. Darkness prevails, and we become blind to our weaknesses and transgressions in that area. However, other people—particularly family—are experts in recognizing and spotting those walls of sin. Because they clearly see the sinful strongholds in our lives, they believe we haven't really been changed by Christ, no matter how loudly we proclaim that we have been. We become our own worst enemies. We may believe that our enemy, the devil, is keeping a family member from Jesus. But in reality, we are the enemy!

Our more assertive family members may even point out the sinful strongholds in our lives. But our hearts have probably been hardened in that area, so we may refuse to listen to them or the conviction of the Holy Spirit in us. Consequently, that stronghold of sin in us keeps an unsaved loved one from seeing the Christ who indwells our Spirit.

IDENTIFYING OUR WALLS

Each of us has walls that keep our unsaved family from seeing Jesus in us. Look over the following list and identify any walls or strongholds that may be blocking your witness for Christ.

- Living in a worldly and immoral manner
- Condemning yourself or others
- Acting one way at church and Christian functions and another way the rest of the time
- Being spiritually arrogant
- Lying, cheating, stealing or not keeping your word
- Avoiding prayer
- Feeling hopeless and depressed
- Lacking love
- Being cynical, critical and derogatory
- Other: _____

4

Now that you are aware of any walls in you, let me tell you that there is hope! We can tear down the walls and let God's light in. The apostle Paul reminded us, "We use God's mighty weapons, not mere worldly weapons, to knock down the Devil's strongholds" (2 Cor. 10:4).

Let's courageously move forward and "knock down" the walls and strongholds within us. Then we can storm the gates and tear down the walls that keep our families from a saving knowledge of Jesus Christ!

CHAPTER 1

THE WALL OF
WORLDLY LIVING

Joan professed to be a sold-out, radical follower of Jesus. She talked often and boldly about how Jesus had saved and changed her. But her family was turned off by the contradictions in her life. Although she no longer lived at home, her family knew about her lifestyle—and her one-night stands. She still went to wild parties and often didn't get home until the next morning.

Joan excused her behavior with the familiar cliché, "Christians aren't perfect, just forgiven." Her lifestyle told them that she believed she could live however she wanted because that didn't matter once you were saved. While Joan's family was unsaved, they had high moral standards and viewed themselves as actually living more moral lives than did Joan, who professed to be a Christian. How could she be "saved" and they be "sinners," as she claimed, when they lived better lives than she did? It should be no surprise, then, to discover that her family members interpreted her religion as "way out there," perhaps even cultish.

Scrutinizing Joan's life didn't lead her family members to a conviction of their own sin or even to the conclusion that God had rescued Joan from hers. After all, Joan still seemed to be as immoral as she was before her conversion. And her immorality loomed huge before their eyes, especially when she talked to them about Christ.

Joan's worldly living was a wall in her life that kept her family from seeing Jesus in her.

LIVING IN THE ENEMY'S CAMP

Joan's life mimicked Lot's spiritual journey in Genesis 13. Remember the story? Abram and his nephew, Lot, had traveled from Egypt up into Canaan. Both had become extremely wealthy, with large families and herds of animals. Eventually the herdsmen of Abram and Lot fought over pasture, wells and places to pitch their tents. So Abram suggested that the two clans go their separate ways.

In deciding where to live, Lot made a choice based on his desires instead of on the wisdom and fear of God. Lot chose the well-watered plains of the Jordan Valley—but in this valley were the cities of Sodom

and Gomorrah, which were strongholds of sinful per-
versions.

Lot was "a righteous man who was distressed by the
wickedness he saw and heard day after day" (2 Pet.
2:8). But while Lot was good, he made some bad
choices that put his family in peril. He lived too close
to the world and saw his family almost destroyed as a
result of it.

Let's look at how Lot led his family right into the
enemy's camp.

1. Gazing at the world

> Lot took a long look at the fertile plains of the
> Jordan Valley in the direction of Zoar. The
> whole area was well watered everywhere, like
> the garden of the LORD or the beautiful land of
> Egypt.
>
> —GENESIS 13:10

Lot chose to fix his eyes on what *looked* good
instead of asking God what *was* good for himself and
his family.

Lot built altars and worshiped the living God with
Abram. He had made the choice to leave his old life
and start a new one in obedience to God. Yet, he still
gazed at the world. His eyes were attracted to carnal
things, and Lot allowed himself to gaze at and long
for them.

Joan had a similar problem. She was still attracted
by the neon lights of worldly pleasures. She mistakenly

thought she could hold on to things from her old life while living her new one. An old hymn of the church says, "I surrender all." But to both Joan and Lot, it would be, "I surrender some."

Neither Lot nor Joan turned their gaze from the world. They failed to guard their hearts or their sight. Lot's family ended up fleeing for their lives from the evil their "spiritual guide" had led them into. Joan was also a spiritual guide for her family because she pointed the way to Christ. But her family would be in harm's way, too, if they followed her lead.

Let's look at our own lives and see if there's any of Lot or Joan in us. Can your family follow your lead? Would you want your family to gaze upon all your eyes see? Would you be comfortable with any unsaved family member reading the books or magazines you read? Gazing at the Internet sites you see? Watching the movies, TV shows or videos you watch? Looking at the opposite sex the way you look at them? When they gaze upon what you gaze upon, are you willing to say to them, "You are looking at life through holy and pure eyes"?

In Proverbs we are lovingly warned:

> Pay attention, my child, to what I say. Listen carefully. Don't lose sight of my words. Let them penetrate deep within your heart, for they bring life and radiant health to anyone who discovers their meaning.
>
> Above all else, guard your heart, for it affects everything you do. Avoid all perverse talk; stay

far from corrupt speech. Look straight ahead,
and fix your eyes on what lies before you. Mark
out a straight path for your feet; then stick to the
path and stay safe.

—PROVERBS 4:20–26

In order for our families to come to know God, we
have to set an example of holy living for them. The
psalmist writes, "Taste and see that the LORD is good.
Oh, the joys of those who trust in him!" (Ps. 34:8). If
your unsaved family members see all that you do, will
they see the Lord? Will they taste His goodness by following your example?

The author of Hebrews gives us some pointed
advice:

> Mark out a straight path for your feet. Then
> those who follow you, though they are weak
> and lame, will not stumble and fall but will
> become strong. Try to live in peace with
> everyone, and seek to live a clean and holy life,
> for those who are not holy will not see the Lord.
>
> —HEBREWS 12:13–14

Lot and Joan led their families down a rocky path
full of places that could cause them to stumble. We
are the spiritual eyes for our unsaved family members. Are we leading them down a safe path to
salvation or a perilous path toward destruction? On
what are we fixing our gaze?

We all know the story of Lot's wife. Unfortunately,
she had learned from her husband to look at the

wrong things. While he resisted the temptation of looking back at the destruction of Sodom, his wife could not obey the angel's command not to look. So she ended up being transformed into a pillar of salt. Her gaze resulted in her destruction.

God's Word tells us where to fix our gaze:

> Therefore, since we are surrounded by such a huge crowd of witnesses to the life of faith, let us strip off every weight that slows us down, especially the sin that so easily hinders our progress. And let us run with endurance the race that God has set before us. We do this by keeping our eyes on Jesus, on whom our faith depends from start to finish.
>
> —HEBREWS 12:1–2

2. Living for ourselves

If we truly desire our families to be saved, then we must live for others instead of ourselves. Selfishness is a wall that keeps others from seeing Christ in us. When we draw attention to ourselves—our desires and wants—then we draw attention away from Jesus.

Lot didn't consider well enough the safety or salvation of his family when he chose where to live. Yes, he may have been strong, good and righteous, but what about his wife and children? Were they as strong as he was? Could they resist temptation as he could? Lot made the choice based on his own desires.

Lot chose that land for himself—the Jordan

Valley to the east of them. He went there with his flocks and servants and parted company with his uncle Abram.

—GENESIS 13:11

Once we belong to Christ, we are no longer to live for ourselves. Paul writes:

Don't you know that your body is the temple of the Holy Spirit, who lives in you and was given to you by God? You do not belong to yourself, for God bought you with a high price. So you must honor God with your body.

—1 CORINTHIANS 6:19–20

Lot made himself the priority in his life. He didn't ask God what he should do. There was no altar built, no prayers prayed, no worship offered and no guidance sought. He simply did what was right in his own eyes. God's people have always ended up plagued by the enemy when they do that. Have you noticed that sometimes your ways are not God's ways? What we would choose for ourselves is often not what God desires for us or our family. The Lord reminds us:

"My thoughts are completely different from yours," says the LORD. "And my ways are far beyond anything you could imagine. For just as the heavens are higher than the earth, so are my ways higher than your ways and my thoughts higher than your thoughts."

—ISAIAH 55:8–9

Our choices not only affect us but also those around us, particularly our family members. No decision is ever made in isolation, without consequences that affect both ourselves and others. So Lot's decisions as well as Joan's had consequences on others. Our choices can actually pave the way for our family's destruction or salvation.

Lot's choice to settle his family near Sodom and later to move them into the city led to a tragic outcome. He and his daughters escaped with only their lives, losing everything. But his wife and his daughters' betrothed died. Why?

> So Lot rushed out to tell his daughters' fiancés, "Quick, get out of the city! The LORD is going to destroy it." But the young men thought he was only joking.
>
> —GENESIS 19:14

When we continually make worldly choices, our unsaved family members regard our faith as a joke. They believe we are not serious about our beliefs. When we don't take our faith seriously, others won't take it seriously either. Do your lost family members really see you making serious choices in the fear of God, or do they see you taking lightly the eternal consequences of life choices?

3. Living too close to the world's edge

Instead of going out to the edge for Jesus, we find ourselves too often walking a tightrope between holiness and worldliness. Lot pitched his tents and put his family right on the edge of sin.

> So while Abram stayed in the land of Canaan, Lot moved his tents to a place near Sodom, among the cities of the plain. The people of this area were unusually wicked and sinned greatly against the LORD.
>
> —GENESIS 13:12–13

While we may have crossed over the Red Sea from Egypt (the world) to the wilderness (walking with God), we may find ourselves like the ancient Israelites longing for the land of slavery and bondage we just left. Instead of distancing ourselves from the world's sins and temptations, we often pitch our family's tent right in the midst of evil.

The wisdom of Proverbs aptly warns and instructs:

> Do not do as the wicked do or follow the path of evildoers. Avoid their haunts. Turn away and go somewhere else, for evil people cannot sleep until they have done their evil deed for the day. They cannot rest unless they have caused someone to stumble. They eat wickedness and drink violence!
>
> The way of the righteous is like the first gleam of dawn, which shines ever brighter until the full light of day. But the way of the wicked is like complete darkness. Those who follow it have no idea what they are stumbling over.
>
> —PROVERBS 4:14–19

Ask yourself about your choices:

- Do you allow unholy TV shows or videos into your home?
- Are there sexually explicit magazines or other offensive materials at home?
- Do you permit profane and unholy music to be played at home?
- Do you use profane or dirty language?
- Are you morally pure in your actions with yourself and others?

If we allow the immorality of the world into our homes, our conversation or our actions, then we become a stumbling block for our family members in coming to know Jesus. Lot was righteous, but he led his family into the midst of temptation and evil. As a result, all of them were lost but his two daughters and him. What a sad commentary that living too close to the edge of the world pushed most of his family into destruction.

TEAR DOWN THE WALL

If the wall of worldly or immoral living blocks your unsaved family members from seeing Jesus in you, then it's time to repent and tear the wall down. You can take practical steps to remove the bricks of sin that have created a worldly stronghold in your life. Remember that the unsaved can clearly see our sinful blind spots. They will often be distracted by those instead of being attracted to God's Spirit living in us.

Practical steps

- Draw near to God and distance yourself from worldly desires and lusts.
- Ask family members to forgive you for the worldly temptations you have exposed them to and graciously accept any revelations about your sin that they may have.
- Put away all malicious or impure talk, gossip, put-downs and vulgarity.
- Remove sensual, sex-oriented, violent and vulgar materials from your home, including magazines, books, videos and materials containing astrological, occult and New Age information.
- Don't become self-righteous or overly pious about your separation from the world. Just indulge in clean, simple living.
- Refuse to condemn your unsaved family members for their impure ways. Instead, lovingly affirm holy alternatives to unholy living.
- Demonstrate holiness by living it instead of talking about it.

Pray

Praying through this wall requires serious self-examination and a desire to live a holy life. Holiness requires us to live a *worthy* life, not a *worldly* life.

Therefore I, a prisoner for serving the Lord, beg you to lead a life *worthy* of your calling, for you have been called by God. Be humble and gentle. Be patient with each other, making allowance for each other's faults because of your love.
                    —EPHESIANS 4:1–2, EMPHASIS ADDED

But whatever happens to me, you must live in a manner *worthy* of the Good News about Christ, as citizens of heaven. Then, whether I come and see you again or only hear about you, I will know that you are standing side by side, fighting together for the Good News.
                    —PHILIPPIANS 1:27, EMPHASIS ADDED

We pleaded with you, encouraged you, and urged you to live your lives in a way that God would consider *worthy.* For he called you into his Kingdom to share his glory.
                    —1 THESSALONIANS 2:12, EMPHASIS ADDED

If you explain this to the others, you will be doing your duty as a *worthy* servant of Christ Jesus, one who is fed by the message of faith and the true teaching you have followed.
                    —1 TIMOTHY 4:6, EMPHASIS ADDED

Michael Brown, president of the Brownsville Revival School of Ministry, makes a fitting observation:

Sin in our lives will take away from our effectiveness here in this world. Sin in our lives will displease the Lord and delight the devil. Sin in our lives will hurt many others—both in this world and in the world to come—and sin in our lives will hurt us too, perhaps forever. But holiness will bring us nothing but good, in this world and in the world to come.[1]

Holiness tears down our wall of worldly living and is an example of purity for our lost family members. We can pray for holiness—or even pray for the desire to be holy. Start wherever you are. You might begin by praying this:

> *Lord, purify me. Expose every impure thought, action, word and attitude in my life. Reveal to me all the unholy things in my life that I am attached to. Give me the desire to purge them from my life. Teach me to walk on Your highway of holiness and to drink from Your fountains of pure and living water. Empower me to be an example of holiness to the unsaved around me, particularly my family. Thank You, Jesus, for Your purifying blood that cleanses me from the stain of sin and keeps me holy. Amen.*

Reach out

Once you have torn down the wall of worldly living, you can begin to reach out to your unsaved family members. Consider these ways:

- Give them pure and godly material to read, view and enjoy. There are many excellent videos, books, CDs and magazines available that will edify your family.
- Speak with holy language. That does not mean pious, superficial, religious talk. It means encouraging language that speaks life, not death, to your family.
- Have good, clean fun with your family. Do things together that everyone can enjoy, things untainted by vulgarity, materialism and sensualism.
- Refuse to argue with family members about New Age or occult materials. Simply eliminate them from your home and your discussions.
- Serve your family members with pure motives. Instead of manipulating them into receiving Christ, give freely to them in order to bless them.
- Live a worthy life—a life worth imitating. Paul writes, "And you should follow my example, just as I follow Christ's" (1 Cor. 11:1). Live an exemplary life without seeking your family's attention or praise for how good you are. Do it for Jesus.

Do you wish your family were saved? Then live from the inside out. Let the indwelling Spirit of God rule your body and soul. Stop allowing the world to influence your behavior, emotions and thoughts. As you begin walking your talk, your family will see a changed person.

Learn from Lot's example. Quit living so close to the

edge of the world that you might fall off the cliff and take yourself and your family down to destruction.

On a recent trip to Yugoslavia to speak at a young adult conference and to teach in a Bible school, I had a college student as an interpreter. One night after a tear-filled and life-changing service, I prayed with him at the altar.

"My father hates me and beats me," he confided. His father was a government official from the old Communist days who despised the fact that his only son had converted to soft, weak Christianity. This cruel father did everything in his power to make his son's life miserable. As a result, a growing offense and bitterness was rising in this young man's heart. Yet he so desired to follow Christ.

"How are you treating your father?" I asked.

"I try to avoid him at all times," he confessed honestly. "My father will only hurt me when I am around him. He knows how I love Jesus, and he tries to keep me away from church every time there is a service."

"Why don't you try simply loving and respecting your father?" I suggested. "Tell him you love him. Ask him how you might pray for him. Above all, let him see that Jesus has given you love for your family, not rejection or hate."

My young friend agreed, and after we prayed together, he left to catch his bus to go across Belgrade to his home.

One year later when my wife and I returned to Yugoslavia, this college student was again my interpreter. He rushed up to me before the service and gave me a huge hug. My first question was, "How are things with your father?"

"Much better," he smiled. "Not long after you prayed with me last year, my father became very ill. For weeks I served him in every way I knew how. I even prayed for him to get well, and his health improved. I have learned how to love him again and how to stop pressuring him about my faith."

We prayed together in agreement that one day his father would accept Jesus. By the way, his new loving attitude did reach his mother, who greeted me that day. She was a new believer in Jesus!

CHAPTER 2

THE WALL OF PRAYERLESSNESS

ohn and Amy were so distraught over their son's rebellion against God, his use of drugs and his complete disrespect of authority that they gave up. They even gave up praying for him.

Their son, Brad, had started hanging around with the wrong crowd at school. His attitude grew defiant, and he refused to comply with curfews. Eventually, he wouldn't follow any household rules at all.

John and Amy had done all the right things. They had taken Brad to church, Sunday school, youth groups, Christian events—they had even enrolled him in Christian school during his elementary years. But Brad had begged to go to public school when he reached junior high. He loved sports, and the Christian school just didn't have the resources or people to put top sport teams on the field. Besides, many of Brad's friends from church went to his school, so it seemed like a safe place.

But Brad was gradually influenced by the wrong people to do the wrong things. At first, John and Amy blamed themselves and tried to pray through the situation with repentance and claiming Brad for Christ. They steadfastly rebuked the devourer and covered Brad with the blood of Christ daily in prayer. The whole family went to Christian counseling, but nothing seemed to help. Brad turned his back on his parents, the church and, more tragically, on Christ.

In high school, problems with the law started. Continual run-ins with the police and a mounting list of juvenile offenses drove a deeper wedge between Brad and his parents. Even the court-ordered curfews, restrictions, probation and short-term disciplinary drug rehab program failed to get Brad's attention. Instead of turning from his ways, he became more hardened and insubordinate. Brad stole what he could from his parents to support his drug habit until finally they forced him to move out of the house.

Eventually, John and Amy stopped doing the most important thing that they could do to help Brad— they stopped praying. Their prayerlessness for Brad arose out of hurt, anger and bitterness—toward Brad, but also toward God for letting this happen. Their impenetrable fortress of pain blocked every word of prayer on Brad's behalf. John and Amy were afraid to hope, and they blamed themselves and God. Praying for Brad was too painful, too raw. What if nothing happened? They just couldn't take any more anguish.

BRICKS THAT COMPRISE THE WALL
OF PRAYERLESSNESS

It's easy to pray when it seems that God answers quickly with a yes! Some seasons of prayer seem so effective that almost the moment a prayer is uttered the answer arrives. During other seasons God's answers seem to come only through our persistence and patience. Other prayers seem to be answered through feverency and fasting. But how shall we pray when nothing seems to work?

In Psalm 77 we have the privilege of watching a man named Asaph privately cry out in anguish to God. So intense is his pain that he is driven to prayerlessness. Much like John and Amy, Asaph declares that he is simply too distressed to pray!

> I cry out to God without holding back.
>   Oh, that God would listen to me!
> When I was in deep trouble,
>   I searched for the LORD.
> All night long I pray, with hands lifted toward
>   heaven, pleading.
>   There can be no joy for me until he acts.
> I think of God, and I moan,
>   overwhelmed with longing for his help.
> You don't let me sleep.

I am too distressed even to pray!

—PSALM 77:1–4

The wall of prayerless is built brick by brick. Let's look at some of the bricks.

Disappointment. When lost loved ones continually disappoint us, we may finally give up on expecting anything positive to happen in their lives—including salvation.

Hurt. It's hard to pray continually for someone who willingly and knowingly keeps hurting and rejecting us. Pain can add many bricks to the wall of prayerlessness.

Indifference. Sometimes loved ones are indifferent toward us and all our efforts to reach them. After a while, their apathy influences us, and we are tempted to become indifferent about the most important thing in their lives—salvation.

Arrogance. There are times when loved ones are so obnoxious that we come to believe that they really have earned a trip to hell. We hate to admit it, but we want to see them get what they deserve.

But aren't we thankful that God isn't giving us what we deserve? In His mercy through Christ, God has given us the free gift of salvation, not the punishment all of us have earned. Yes, our proud, arrogant loved ones may deserve hell—but so do you and I! We can't let their arrogance turn us off from praying.

Whatever has tempted us to add bricks to our wall of prayerlessness, the truth is that we don't have a choice to quit praying for the lost, including our loved ones. Prayerlessness is simply not an option for us as believers. Scripture clearly commands, "Keep on praying" (1 Thess. 5:17).

WHY IS PRAYER EFFECTIVE AND ESSENTIAL?

It's important for us to tear down the wall of prayerlessness. Why? Because the very thing the enemy desires is that we stop praying. In many instances the only way a lost family member will be reached with the gospel is through prayer.

Pastor Jack Hayford insightfully comments, "Prayer is essentially a partnership of the redeemed child of God [that's you!] working hand in hand with God toward the realization of His redemptive purposes [one of which is the salvation of your family] on earth."[1]

The fact that we don't pray does not nullify the atoning work of Jesus on the cross. He died to save the lost, and it's God's will that all be saved. But our neglecting to pray for our family could be the very thing that stands between them and God.

How can that be? Peter Wagner has written, "Human inaction does not nullify the atonement, but human inaction can make the atonement ineffective for lost people."[2] When we fail to pray, there is a deficit of workers for the harvest. Jesus commanded, "The harvest is so great, but the workers are so few. So pray to the Lord who is in charge of the harvest; ask him to send out more workers for his fields" (Matt. 9:37–38).

Consider this. While we may not personally be able

to reach a lost family member, somebody else can. A department store clerk, a coworker, a neighbor, a coach or a teammate may be just the person God can use to reach a lost family member. So how will they be prompted to witness to that lost family member? By our prayers!

God has established prayer as the means by which His people effect His will on earth. Jesus taught us to pray for God's will to be done "on earth as it is in heaven" (Matt. 6:10, NKJV). So our prayers inspired by the Spirit of God will raise up workers to reach the lost.

Neglecting to pray means that fewer and fewer believers will cross the path of our lost family members. Fewer witnesses will be prompted to share the gospel with that son, that daughter, that father or mother or brother or sister. Our prayers activate the perfect climate in which the Spirit can move to bring countless believers into our lost loved ones' lives. Those believers will be used as vessels in God's hands to share the gospel with them.

So we must pray for a relentless flood of harvest workers to cross paths with our lost loved ones. Pray that boldness will fill each of them with just the right words to share to touch those hardened, lost hearts. Pray that at just the right moment—during a divine appointment—our loved ones will be convicted by the Spirit to accept Christ. Pray!

TEAR DOWN THE WALL

Sometimes we may feel overwhelmed and too distressed to pray. That's exactly what the enemy wants. Satan desires us to remain prayerless so that fewer workers will go to the lost—including our lost family members. If we find ourselves collapsed behind a wall of prayerlessness, then we need to try some of the following ways to come back to spiritual life and begin praying again. If you feel too overcome to do much, just pick one of these steps and do it faithfully, regardless of your feelings. The feelings will come as you start praying again.

Practical steps

- Ask God to forgive you for not praying.

  Lord Jesus, I am sorry for spending too little time with You in prayer. I ask Your Spirit to pray in me and through me, especially for my lost loved ones. Help me to become disciplined in my daily prayer time. As I pray, fill me with hope and joy over the coming salvation of my lost loved ones. Amen.

- Find a prayer partner who will pray and agree with you at regular times for the salvation of your lost ones. Start with once a week, then make it more often.

Tearing down the wall of prayerlessness will likely require the help of a prayer partner. When we are prayerless, it's too easy to make excuses for why we don't pray. Someone who loves the Lord needs to hold us accountable for praying. I have an early morning prayer partner who connects with me often. He calls me or I call him every morning at a set time, like 6:00 or 7:00 A.M. Then we share a scripture and pray together. This allows us to remain constant and accountable in our prayer time.

- Keep a spiritual journal and write down all your prayer requests so that you can see how God is answering your prayers.

Pray

Praying scriptures about prayer is an effective and powerful way to get back into the habit of prayer. It will renew your mind toward prayer and release power in the spiritual realm at the same time, because God's Word is alive and full of power (Heb. 4:12). Pray these passages about prayer regularly, personalizing them as you do. If you pray them often, you will automatically memorize them, and your prayer life will be off to a running start!

> Then if my people who are called by my name will humble themselves and pray and seek my face and turn from their wicked ways, I will hear from heaven and will forgive their sins and heal their land.
>
> —2 CHRONICLES 7:14

I am praying to you because I know you will
    answer, O God.
Bend down and listen as I pray.
—PSALM 17:6

Through each day the LORD pours his unfailing
    love upon me,
    and through each night I sing his songs,
    praying to God who gives me life.
—PSALM 42:8

But I keep right on praying to you, LORD,
    hoping this is the time you will show me
    favor.
In your unfailing love, O God,
    answer my prayer with your sure salvation.
Pull me out of the mud;
    don't let me sink any deeper!
Rescue me from those who hate me,
    and pull me from these deep waters.
Don't let the floods overwhelm me,
    or the deep waters swallow me,
    or the pit of death devour me.
Answer my prayers, O LORD,
    for your unfailing love is wonderful.
Turn and take care of me,
    for your mercy is so plentiful.
—PSALM 69:13–16

I love the LORD because he hears
    and answers my prayers.

Because he bends down and listens,
I will pray as long as I have breath!
—PSALM 116:1–2

So pray to the Lord who is in charge of the harvest;
ask him to send out more workers for his fields.
—MATTHEW 9:38

God knows how often I pray for you. Day and
night I bring you and your needs in prayer to
God, whom I serve with all my heart by telling
others the Good News about his Son.
—ROMANS 1:9

And the Holy Spirit helps us in our distress. For
we don't even know what we should pray for,
nor how we should pray. But the Holy Spirit
prays for us with groanings that cannot be
expressed in words. And the Father who knows
all hearts knows what the Spirit is saying, for the
Spirit pleads for us believers in harmony with
God's own will. And we know that God causes
everything to work together for the good of
those who love God and are called according
to his purpose for them.
—ROMANS 8:26–28

Pray at all times and on every occasion in the
power of the Holy Spirit. Stay alert and be persistent in your prayers for all Christians everywhere.
—EPHESIANS 6:18

Don't worry about anything; instead, pray about everything. Tell God what you need, and thank him for all he has done.

—Philippians 4:6

God wants to help us overcome prayerlessness. We only have to ask. Remember to expect this prayer to be answered when you pray:

Spirit of God, dismantle my wall of prayerlessness with a zeal to pray for workers in Your harvest of souls. Particularly help me pray for my lost loved ones even when I am disappointed, hurt, indifferent or turned off by them. Fill me with a compassion for them. Give hope when I feel hopeless about their conversion. And most of all, when I don't know how to pray for them, pray through me by Your Spirit. Amen.

Reach out

Once you begin pulling down the wall of prayerlessness, you can focus your prayers for your lost loved ones in these ways:

- Pray for each lost loved one by name, asking the Holy Spirit to prepare each heart to listen to the gospel and to receive it.
- Pray for believers to cross their paths daily wherever they work, play, live and shop.
- Pray for believers to be bold to share the gospel with your lost loved ones.
- Pray for personal boldness and wisdom in

sharing the gospel with them.
- Ask God to give you the patience to pray for your lost family members for as long as it takes for them to be saved.
- Refuse to let your feelings or circumstances dictate when and how you pray for your family. Keep praying, believing that they will come to Christ. Claim His promise, "You didn't choose me. I chose you. I appointed you to go and produce fruit that will last, so that the Father will give you whatever you ask for, using my name" (John 15:16).

Do you wish your family members were saved? Then pray. Pray God's will for their salvation. Pray for workers in the harvest of souls. And listen to the prompting of the Holy Spirit to witness to others. Remember that the people you witness to are other people's loved ones. You may be an answer to their prayers when you reach out to their loved ones for Jesus.

God's will is that your lost loved ones will come to know Him and that you will pray for them. Keep praying, and refuse to let the wall of prayerlessness keep your family from being saved!

CHAPTER 3

THE WALL OF CONDEMNATION

A t first, Miriam's radical, life-changing conversion was a curiosity to her unsaved family and
friends. She seemed so excited and full of life.
Then she marched into her family's lives like
Alexander the Great. Taking no prisoners, she sought
to convert every family member. Those who would
not convert she wrote off as incorrigible sinners, lost
forever to the flames of hell.

Most of her family were offended at her brash
actions and overbearing attitude. She exhibited no
compassion—only condemnation and judgment.
She was quick to point out the sins of everyone in the
family. Yet Miriam's past sinful ways were still fresh in

their memories. Though they recognized that she had indeed left her wild past, she seemed to have traded it in for a lifestyle that condemned them for what she had just been living! Her wall of condemnation turned her family off and shut them out.

Miriam's teenage son was particularly affected. He dreaded her endless lectures on how evil his music, video games and friends were. He avoided bringing any of his friends home for fear that she would first condemn them, then try forcibly to convert them. Instead of leading her son to Christ, Miriam's condemnation was doing just the opposite—driving him away.

CONDEMNATION DRIVES FAMILY AWAY FROM JESUS

Condemning the wrong in others turns them off to both us and Jesus. Jesus strongly rebuked the religious, self-righteous of His day, but He never condemned sinners. The most famous scripture of all confirms this:

> For God so loved the world that he gave his only Son, so that everyone who believes in him will not perish but have eternal life. God did not send his Son into the world to condemn it, but to save it.
>
> —JOHN 3:16–17

Condemnation communicates that an unsaved person has no worth, no dignity and no importance to God or Christians. The truth is that God loved sinners so much and valued sinners so highly that He gave His only Son to die for them—and that includes us. We were lost sinners before He redeemed us. Christ didn't condemn us while we were sinners, and we have no right to condemn our family members who are living in sin.

The Greek word for "condemn," *krino,* means "to judge and assign an eternal damnation" to a person. We must understand that the right to judge or condemn doesn't belong to us. It belongs solely to God. Our job is to convey the love of the Father. Love attracts love. Mercy encourages conviction and confession. That's the attitude we need to communicate to our lost family members.

In the New Testament, the self-righteous, religious leaders freely condemned those they regarded as terrible sinners. Yet Jesus loved sinners and rebuked those who had a condemning attitude.

> The teachers of religious law and the Pharisees are the official interpreters of the Scriptures. So practice and obey whatever they say to you, but don't follow their example. For they don't practice what they teach. They crush you with impossible religious demands and never lift a finger to help ease the burden. Everything they do is for show.
>
> —MATTHEW 23:2–5

We often condemn in others what we are (or have been) guilty of in our own lives. So before we are quick to condemn unsaved family members for their sins, we should carefully examine our own lives. As we judge others, so we will be judged.

> Stop judging others, and you will not be judged. For others will treat you as you treat them. Whatever measure you use in judging others, it will be used to measure how you are judged.
>
> —MATTHEW 7:1–2

The good news is that we can ask God to fill us with His mercy and forgiving love for our family members instead of condemning them. They need to hear Good News of His love from us, not the bad news about their sin.

SELF-CONDEMNATION KEEPS FAMILY FROM CHRIST

Continually putting ourselves down can also be a wall keeping our family from Christ. On the one hand, we tell ourselves that we can do all things through Christ who strengthens us (Phil. 4:13). On the other hand, we confess that we are inadequate and unable to keep a job, pay our bills, discipline our children, love our enemies, serve others and stay physically healthy.

In other words, our family does not see the power of the gospel at work in us. So, they reason that if God's saving power doesn't work in our lives, it cannot work in theirs either. Instead of our family seeing us built up in Christ, they see self-condemnation tearing us down and making us powerless to live abundant lives in Christ (John 10:10).

Self-condemnation renders us powerless and ineffective witnesses. What kind of a witness is it to our lost family members if we say that God loves us, but we have a hard time loving ourselves? Either Jesus Christ has made a radical difference in our lives and everything is changed, or we are simply spitting into the wind. Scripture forcefully declares:

> So now there is no condemnation for those who belong to Christ Jesus. For the power of the life-giving Spirit has freed you through Christ Jesus from the power of sin that leads to death.
> —ROMANS 8:1–2

When our witness to our lost family members is blocked by self-criticism, they cannot see the power of God's love either at work in us or through us. And, based on the condemnation they see in us, they may believe that God is a hard taskmaster.

TEAR DOWN THE WALL

Laying a guilt trip on ourselves or others in our family builds the wall of condemnation in our relationships. Condemnation communicates rejection. When we condemn, we reject others who do not meet or live up to our standards or the righteousness of God.

As long as we judge, criticize, reject and condemn

our lost family members, we will never reach them with the love of Christ. The good news is that in response to our failures, God provided a way of reconciliation through the cross of Jesus Christ. We have been called to be ambassadors of reconciliation—not condemnation.

> For God was in Christ, reconciling the world to himself, no longer counting people's sins against them. This is the wonderful message he has given us to tell others. We are Christ's ambassadors, and God is using us to speak to you. We urge you, as though Christ himself were here pleading with you, "Be reconciled to God!" For God made Christ, who never sinned, to be the offering for our sin, so that we could be made right with God through Christ.
> —2 CORINTHIANS 5:19–21

Being an ambassador of reconciliation does not mean that we compromise holiness or tolerate sin. Jesus has provided the perfect example for this. When a woman was caught in adultery and brought to Jesus by the religious leaders who wanted to stone her, Jesus reminded them that they too had sin in their lives by inviting any without sin to cast the first stone at her. Once the woman's accusers dropped their stones and left, Jesus said to the adulterous woman:

> "Where are your accusers? Didn't even one of them condemn you?"

"No, Lord," she said.

And Jesus said, "Neither do I. Go and sin no more."

—John 8:10–11

Are you willing to treat your lost family members the way Jesus treated this woman? The antidote to the poisonous stings of condemnation is the balm of Gilead (Jer. 8:22)—the forgiving love of Jesus Christ.

Practical steps

You may be under the teaching or preaching of someone who is condemning and judgmental. One way to tear down the wall of condemnation is to stop accepting the teaching of condemnation and instead put yourself under the gospel message of reconciliation. Robert S. McGee, in *Search for Significance*, has an important insight on this subject:

> Many misguided preachers have used rejection and guilt as a forceful means of motivation. They expound upon our weaknesses, our failures, our unworthiness, and our inability to measure up to Christ's high standards. Not only is our performance declared unworthy, but we are left feeling denounced, devalued, and devastated. As a result, thousands who have been broken by this rejection have left the church without understanding God's accepting, unconditional love, a love that never uses condemnation to correct behavior.[1]

If you have been condemned, you are more likely to condemn others. If you are motivated by guilt, you are more likely to motivate your lost loved ones by pointing out the guilt (or creating it!) in their lives. In order to tear down the wall of condemnation, you need to:

- Accept for yourself the good news of God's reconciling love through Christ Jesus.
- Believe that you are not under condemnation.
- Accept and love your lost family members as God loves them. You can take a firm stand against sin without condemning the sinner.
- Refuse to sit under condemning preaching or teaching. Find a community of believers who are ambassadors of reconciliation, not conveyers of condemnation.
- See yourself and your family members through the lens of God's incomparable love, which imparts worthiness, not worthlessness. Hear the loving Father say, "I have loved you, my people, with an everlasting love. With unfailing love I have drawn you to myself" (Jer. 31:3).

Pray

Praying down the wall of condemnation will require two steps:

1. Pray to receive God's uncondemning and unconditional love for yourself. This prayer adapted from Romans 8 may help you:

Lord Jesus, thank You for removing all condemnation from my life through Your blood that was shed on the cross of Calvary. I declare that I belong to You. I declare that through faith in You, there is no condemnation in me. By Your grace I receive the life-giving Holy Spirit, who fills me with power and breaks the bondage of sin in my life. Thank You, Jesus, for loving me. Enable me to love others and myself with Your unconditional love. Amen.

2. Ask Christ to teach you to love instead of condemning, judging or criticizing those in your family, including those who are lost. To tear down the wall of condemnation toward them, I invite you to pray this prayer adapted from 1 Corinthians 13 (insert name of lost family member):

God's love in and through me for _____ is patient and kind. God's love in and through me for _____ is not jealous or boastful or proud. God's love in and through me for _____ does not demand its own way. God's love in and through me for _____ is not irritable, and it keeps no record of when it has been wronged. God's love in and through me for _____ is never glad about injustice, but rejoices whenever the truth wins out. God's love in and through me for _____ never gives up, never loses faith, is always

hopeful, and endures through every circum-
stance. God's love in and through me for
_____ *will last forever. Amen.*

Pray this regularly—perhaps daily—for your lost family members. Not only will this prayer declare the reconciling love of God to your ears and to the enemy's, it will also open the door for God to remove all condemnation from your life.

Try praying this prayer for yourself as well. For example, "God's love for me is patient and kind." Decide today to declare, receive and share this message of reconciliation from the Father.

Reach out

After tearing down the wall of condemnation, reach out to your unsaved family members by:

- Finding practical ways to demonstrate your love to them. Remember them on their birthdays and holidays. Surprise them with encouraging cards, notes or e-mails.
- Affirming what they do right instead of condemning what they do wrong.
- Telling them how God loves them unconditionally.
- Asking their forgiveness for the times you have condemned or judged them.
- Refusing to be offended when they do something of which you disapprove.
- Rejecting the irrational and unholy belief that people (including yourself) who act in ways

you disapprove of are bad, and they deserve blame and punishment.

· Guarding your tongue so that you only speak life and not death to family members. Before you are tempted to criticize, judge or condemn, pray, "Father, let me say only what You would have me say by the power of Your love. Amen."

Do you wish that your family would get saved? Then stop condemning them and start loving them instead. Nail your judgmental attitudes to the cross and let the love of Christ control you. Take courage that you can be changed from the example of Saul (before he became the apostle Paul). He hated early Christians so much that he hunted them down and killed them. He condemned and judged others to the extreme! But notice what God did in his life:

> How thankful I am to Christ Jesus our Lord for considering me trustworthy and appointing me to serve him, even though I used to scoff at the name of Christ. I hunted down his people, harming them in every way I could. But God had mercy on me because I did it in ignorance and unbelief. Oh, how kind and gracious the Lord was! He filled me completely with faith and the love of Christ Jesus.
>
> —1 TIMOTHY 1:12–14

Ask Jesus right now to fill you completely with His faith and love so that your lost family members will encounter Christ's love in you!

CHAPTER 4

THE WALL OF
UNBELIEF

H ave you ever dreamed about what it will be like at the judgment seat of Christ? How about at the final judgment? I have, and I want to share it with you now.

In my dream, the saints of all the ages stood worshiping at the throne of the Lamb. But two sounds mingled mysteriously together at His throne—the strains of heavenly choruses and the noise of sorrowful sobbings. I had never heard any earthly sounds to compare with this unearthly concert of millions of voices singing and sobbing.

The scene then compressed, zooming in to a close-up shot of a figure moving through the masses. The

Son of Man paused before each saint, looking for a moment at the person, then turning His gaze to the offering of objects at each saint's feet. As in the hymn "The Old Rugged Cross," each pile seemed to be the accumulated "trophies" that the saint was presenting to Jesus. I remembered the promise of God's Word that God's people would be given crowns in heaven. But prior to Jesus passing by, only the heap of life's trophies were lying there.

Somehow I saw Jesus look into the eyes of one unnamed saint. His eyes were far from nondescript. They blazed with an eternal fire, made intense with passionate love and penetrating judgment. When His gaze went from that saint's eyes to his offering, immediately the offering burst into flames.

In front of some saints, all that remained of their life's treasures was an ashen heap of black, smoldering cinders. This startling revealing of the worthlessness of their treasures brought deep sobs and weeping that filled the air with mournful strains of sad remorse. Tears flooded down their cheeks and soaked their white linen robes.

The life treasures of all the saints were burned. Some had only ashes left, but the fire left others with priceless crowns and jewels of infinite worth. (See 1 Corinthians 3:12–15.) These saints responded with jubilant choruses of praise and thanksgiving.

The scene in my dream then changed. I found myself standing with an uncountable number of saints at the final judgment seat of God. I realized that the focus of this judgment was not the saints, but those standing across a fiery abyss. To my chagrin and horror, I recognized some of the faces. I saw work associates and neighbors, people who had served me over the years. Family members and relatives were among that throng as well. My heart broke, and tears overflowed from within me and flooded my entire being.

The look in the eyes of my doomed family members and relatives spoke more sorrow and suffering than any I had ever seen. Their eyes tragically asked, "Why didn't you tell me? Why didn't you try harder? Why did you give up on me?" Oh, the unspeakable sadness...

THE GLORY OF HEAVEN AND THE HORROR OF HELL

Because we as believers hear about heaven often, we tend to allow familiarity and the assurance of our salvation to dim our vision of heaven—and hell. If heaven is as glorious as God's Word declares—and it is—then why wouldn't we zealously and continually tell everyone about it? If hell is as bad as Jesus described, why don't we warn those we love?

Let's examine our beliefs a moment. Do we really believe that hell and heaven exist eternally? Are we convinced that those trusting Jesus will go to heaven while those rejecting Him will go to hell? If we do, then why would we passively sit by and allow those we love to miss heaven and end up in hell? Would we want to look at the end of time across that fiery lake of hell into the face of a loved one destined to spend eternity in hell?

Jesus believed in a real hell.

> So if your eye—even if it is your good eye—causes you to lust, gouge it out and throw it away. It is better for you to lose one part of your body than for your whole body to be thrown into hell. And if your hand—even if it is your stronger hand—causes you to sin, cut it off and throw it away. It is better for you to lose one part of your body than for your whole body to be thrown into hell.
>
> —MATTHEW 5:29–30

> Don't be afraid of those who want to kill you. They can only kill your body; they cannot touch your soul. Fear only God, who can destroy both soul and body in hell.
>
> —MATTHEW 10:28

> I, the Son of Man, will send my angels, and they will remove from my Kingdom everything that causes sin and all who do evil, and they will throw them into the furnace and burn them. There will be weeping and gnashing of teeth. Then the godly will shine like the sun in their Father's Kingdom. Anyone who is willing to hear should listen and understand!
>
> —MATTHEW 13:41–43

Then the king said to his aides, "Bind him hand and foot and throw him out into the outer darkness, where there is weeping and gnashing of teeth." For many are called, but few are chosen.

—MATTHEW 22:13–14

And he will answer, "I assure you, when you refused to help the least of these my brothers and sisters, you were refusing to help me." And they will go away into eternal punishment, but the righteous will go into eternal life.

—MATTHEW 25:45–46

On the other hand, Jesus simply described heaven as being home with Him:

Don't be troubled. You trust God, now trust in me. There are many rooms in my Father's home, and I am going to prepare a place for you. If this were not so, I would tell you plainly. When everything is ready, I will come and get you, so that you will always be with me where I am. And you know where I am going and how to get there.

—JOHN 14:1–4

And the apostle John describes his revelation of heaven:

So he took me in spirit to a great, high mountain, and he showed me the holy city, Jerusalem, descending out of heaven from

God. It was filled with the glory of God and sparkled like a precious gem, crystal clear like jasper. Its walls were broad and high, with twelve gates guarded by twelve angels. And the names of the twelve tribes of Israel were written on the gates. There were three gates on each side—east, north, south, and west. The wall of the city had twelve foundation stones, and on them were written the names of the twelve apostles of the Lamb.

The angel who talked to me held in his hand a gold measuring stick to measure the city, its gates, and its wall. When he measured it, he found it was a square, as wide as it was long. In fact, it was in the form of a cube, for its length and width and height were each 1,400 miles. Then he measured the walls and found them to be 216 feet thick (the angel used a standard human measure).

The wall was made of jasper, and the city was pure gold, as clear as glass. The wall of the city was built on foundation stones inlaid with twelve gems: the first was jasper, the second sapphire, the third agate, the fourth emerald, the fifth onyx, the sixth carnelian, the seventh chrysolite, the eighth beryl, the ninth topaz, the tenth chrysoprase, the eleventh jacinth, the twelfth amethyst.

The twelve gates were made of pearls—each gate from a single pearl! And the main street was pure gold, as clear as glass.

No temple could be seen in the city, for the

Lord God Almighty and the Lamb are its temple. And the city has no need of sun or moon, for the glory of God illuminates the city, and the Lamb is its light. The nations of the earth will walk in its light, and the rulers of the world will come and bring their glory to it. Its gates never close at the end of day because there is no night. And all the nations will bring their glory and honor into the city. Nothing evil will be allowed to enter—no one who practices shameful idolatry and dishonesty—but only those whose names are written in the Lamb's Book of Life.

—Revelation 21:10–27

Honestly ask yourself:

- Have I lost my vision of heaven and hell?
- Do I really understand the horrific consequences of a lost family member spending eternity in hell?
- Do I really grasp how glorious and awesome heaven will be for a lost family member who gets saved?
- Do I truly believe that Jesus is the only way to heaven? (See John 14:6.)

No One Is Ever Beyond Reach

The wall of unbelief keeps us from sharing the gospel with our lost loved ones. Not only unbelief in the reality of the glory of heaven and the horror of hell, but also unbelief in the ability of God to save a particular, incorrigible family member.

You may have a family member who is regarded as your family's black sheep. Another loved one may be so bound to drugs or alcohol, the occult, immorality or other terrible sins that you believe him or her to be irretrievably lost. How can you be sure of that? No one is beyond the reach of God!

God's presence is everywhere. Our family members are not in a physical, emotional or spiritual place in which God is absent. God is right there with them. The psalmist declares:

> I can never escape from your spirit!
> I can never get away from your presence!
> If I go up to heaven, you are there;
>   if I go down to the place of the dead,
>   you are there.
> If I ride the wings of the morning,
>   if I dwell by the farthest oceans,
>   even there your hand will guide me,
>   and your strength will support me.
> —PSALM 139:7–10

God's love is infinite. We cannot fathom the expanse and prodigality of His love. Amazingly, God doesn't love you or me now any more or less than the moment we accepted Jesus as our Lord and Savior. Beyond that, God doesn't love our lost family members less than He loves us. His *agape* love is unconditional and eternal. Since His love is a gift received by grace, neither you nor I nor any other person, including lost loved ones, can earn His love. Ponder this:

> I pray that Christ will be more and more at home in your hearts as you trust in him. May your roots go down deep into the soil of God's marvelous love. And may you have the power to understand, as all God's people should, how wide, how long, how high, and how deep his love really is.
>
> —EPHESIANS 3:17–18

God seeks out the lost. While our lost loved ones may have no desire to seek or find God, God hasn't given up on them. God has a compassionate heart for the lost. Like a shepherd seeking a lost sheep, our loving Father goes after our lost loved ones.

> If you had one hundred sheep, and one of them strayed away and was lost in the wilderness, wouldn't you leave the ninety-nine others to go and search for the lost one until you found it? And then you would joyfully carry it home on your shoulders. When you arrived, you would call together your friends and neighbors to rejoice with you because your lost sheep was found. In the same way, heaven will be happier over one lost sinner who returns to God than over ninety-nine others who are righteous and haven't strayed away!
>
> —LUKE 15:4–7

Be encouraged and comforted! Nothing any of our lost family members can do or say will make God stop loving them. If God doesn't give up, we shouldn't either. So don't stop praying, sharing, loving and witnessing to your lost family members.

For years several of my family members have been lost. Although they have rejected every attempt I have made to share Jesus with them, I still believe, pray and trust God for their salvation. As long as I have breath, I will believe and claim God's perfect will for them—that they come to a saving knowledge of Jesus Christ as Lord and Savior!

TEAR DOWN THE WALL

Tearing down the wall of unbelief begins with truly believing that Jesus is the only way of salvation. There are no shortcuts or alternate lifestyles—He is the way, the truth and the life; no one comes to the Father except through Him (John 14:6). If you have doubts or unbelief about your relationship with Jesus Christ, let me invite you to pray this right now:

> *Lord Jesus, I confess my doubts and sin. I ask You to forgive me. Fill my mind and heart with Your peace and the knowledge of the truth. Help my unbelief. I believe that You are the way, the truth and the life. You are the Son of God. I receive You as my Lord and Savior. Thank You, Jesus. Amen.*

Practical steps

- Read every passage in the Bible describing heaven and hell, using a concordance or *Nave's Topical Bible* to find them.
- Write down a description of heaven and hell using your own words. Share it with family members.
- Discuss with your lost family members what they believe about heaven and hell. Help them compare their beliefs with what Scripture teaches.
- Examine your heart. Has your zeal for Jesus waned? Are you as excited about going to heaven as you were when you were first saved? Ask Christ to rekindle your zeal.
- Confess aloud these scriptures that declare the everlasting love of God, believing them for your lost loved ones: John 3:16; 14:1–6; 1 John 4:4–13.
- Read Jonathan Edward's classic sermon, "Sinners in the Hands of an Angry God" (available in most bookstores).
- Read Dante's classic, *Inferno*, or study about heaven and hell with Group's Active Curriculum, *Heaven and Hell* (Loveland, CO: Group Publishing, 1992).

Pray

Praying through this wall of unbelief requires a reality check in our spiritual lives. Too often, we become so comfortable with earthly life that we forget about eternal life. We become so secure in our salvation that we push out of sight the reality of hell for those who are lost. We need to allow the Holy Spirit to rekindle our zeal for evangelism and the urgency to reach our lost loved ones. No one has the assurance that physical life will continue beyond the next breath. So we must pray:

> *Lord Jesus, give me a daily, vivid view of both heaven and hell. Keep eternity on my mind. Fill me with an urgency to reach my lost loved ones. Remove from me any despair, hopelessness or faithlessness about the possibility of reaching them. I believe, Lord, that with You all things are possible, especially the salvation of my lost family members. Remove me from my comfort zone and into the faith zone of telling others about Your wonderful gift of heaven and eternal life. Amen.*

Reach out

Once you have torn down this wall of unbelief, you can reach out to your family members by:

- Giving them a New Testament to read for themselves.
- Sharing with them a book about heaven and hell.
- Asking them their beliefs about life after death.
- Writing a letter to them describing what the Bible says about heaven and hell.
- Writing down your own testimony, making

copies of it and sharing it with both family and friends. A friend of mine who is a physician was soberly reminded of the temporality of life when his close friend and patient suddenly died. As a result, he printed a little booklet of his testimony, titled *Do You Know Him?* In this booklet, he not only shared how Jesus had saved him, but also how the reader can accept Christ. You can do the same.

- Taking time to sit down and read the Book of Revelation from start to finish. Claim this promise for yourself: "God blesses the one who reads this prophecy to the church, and he blesses all who listen to it and obey what it says. For the time is near when these things will happen" (Rev. 1:3).

Do you wish your lost family members would get saved? Then recapture a vivid vision of heaven and hell. Refuse to believe that any lost person is beyond the reach of God's love. And start talking about life — eternal life, that is—with everyone you meet.

CHAPTER 5

THE WALL
OF FEAR

W henever Tom tried to witness to his lost brother, a lump rose in his throat, and panic caused his heart to race. William, Tom's brother, had a Ph.D. in philosophy and loved to argue about religion. That made Tom feel inadequate and just plain stupid.

William always raised questions about Christianity that Tom had never considered. So Tom quickly retreated, asking well-rehearsed standby questions like, "If you were to die tonight, would you go to heaven?"

William would immediately derail the conversation, asking, "How do you know that there's a heaven?

Is there life after death? How do you know that the Bible is any more valid than the Hindu Vedas or the Muslim Koran? How can you defend Christianity when the Bible is filled with historical inconsistencies? If God truly loves us, why do innocent children suffer and die?"

The questions went on and on. Tom feared saying the wrong things or giving poor answers. He also was afraid of appearing ignorant. Finally, he worried that if he kept bringing up the subject of William's salvation, William would become offended and simply reject him. Tom didn't handle rejection very well, especially coming from his older brother, whom he both admired and respected. So Tom backed off completely from sharing his faith further.

WHAT ARE OUR FEARS?

The wall of fear keeps us from sharing Jesus with lost family members. What do you fear most?

- Fear of being rejected
- Fear of not knowing what to say or saying the wrong thing
- Fear of appearing to be ignorant, foolish or stupid
- Fear of being shamed by a family member
- Fear of: _____

The power of God's Spirit can help us overcome every fear. Scripture promises:

> For God has not given us a spirit of fear and
> timidity, but of power, love, and self-discipline.
> So you must never be ashamed to tell others
> about our Lord.
>
> —2 TIMOTHY 1:7–8

Let's look specifically at each type of fear and discover how the Holy Spirit helps us triumph over that fear when witnessing to others.

THE FEAR OF BEING REJECTED

No one likes rejection. Most of us enjoy being loved and affirmed by the significant people in our lives—family, colleagues at work and other believers. But what if lost loved ones so dislike hearing about Jesus that our relationship with them hangs in the balance? We may feel that if we try one more time to witness, they will not only reject Christ, but also reject us.

By the way, it's important to mention here that I'm not talking about rejection we receive because we have tried to cram Jesus down their throats. There is no indication in the New Testament that Jesus or any apostle did that. No, we are to love and serve—plus tell the Good News.

If you have a fear of rejection, here are some ideas that may help.

If possible, don't end communication with a lost loved one because of rejection.

A broken relationship blocks our ability to share Jesus. It's important to do everything possible to maintain a loving, positive relationship with all family members—saved or unsaved. There may be those who reject us simply because we believe in Jesus. They may threaten to reject us if we ever mention Jesus. Remember, that becomes their problem, not ours. We cannot be responsible for their rejection if we have done all we can do to reach out with God's love and grace.

Jesus talked about the rejection that comes from being persecuted for righteousness' sake.

> God blesses you when you are mocked and persecuted and lied about because you are my followers. Be happy about it! Be very glad! For a great reward awaits you in heaven. And remember, the ancient prophets were persecuted, too.
>
> —Matthew 5:11–12

Jesus also told us that some in our families may reject us because of our faith in Him. Even Jesus' own family were estranged from Him:

> There was a crowd around Jesus, and someone said, "Your mother and your brothers and sisters are outside, asking for you."
>
> Jesus replied, "Who is my mother? Who are my brothers?" Then he looked at those around him and said, "These are my mother and brothers. Anyone who does God's will is my brother and sister and mother."
>
> —Mark 3:32–35

Jesus predicted that some would completely reject us to the point that we might have to allow a broken relationship.

> "When you enter each village, be a guest in only one home," he said. "And if a village won't welcome you or listen to you, shake off its dust from your feet as you leave. It is a sign that you have abandoned that village to its fate." So the disciples went out, telling all they met to turn from their sins.
>
> —Mark 6:10–12

We must do what we can to keep communication going. But some believers pride themselves in being rejected by unsaved family members. Yet, their rejection had nothing to do with boldly proclaiming Christ and everything to do with being boneheads. They were ugly, self-righteous and downright obnoxious. Such a witness does not glorify or honor Jesus. Be a humble, loving servant to your lost family members. Then if they reject you, they will also be rejecting the Suffering Servant whom you serve and honor.

With all this in mind, remember:

- Don't be obstinate, unloving, unkind or too aggressive with your witness. Anyone would reject that behavior.
- Don't seek rejection and then wear it like a badge of honor.
- Do everything possible to demonstrate the love of Christ to your lost family members.

- Don't be surprised or disappointed if they choose to reject you because you are a Christian.

Don't stop trying—even if you are rejected.

Rejection is not the ticket to giving up on your lost family members. Jesus was rejected by everyone—including His disciples! Yet He still loved them enough to go to the cross for them. We have to die to ourselves, to our expectations and to our own agendas when we experience rejection from our family members. But we must suffer through it for their sakes.

Too often we want them saved in our way, in our timing, at our convenience and for our glory. When things don't go according to our plans, we use their rejection as our excuse to quit.

Even when we are rejected, we must keep on praying, reaching out in love and seeking to serve them. You may protest that loving those who don't appreciate your love is like casting pearls before swine. Not so! Loving those who don't appreciate your wish for them to get saved is being like Jesus. He died on the cross before anyone appreciated Him or His sacrifice. Are you willing to follow the example of Christ on the cross and die to self for your unsaved loved ones? Paul has set the example for us:

> I myself no longer live, but Christ lives in me. So
> I live my life in this earthly body by trusting in

the Son of God, who loved me and gave himself
for me.

—GALATIANS 2:20

Dying to self is the key to overcoming rejection.

Don't reject them if they reject you.

Our lost loved ones may reject us and break the
relationship. They may feel that they have the right to
take up the bait of Satan and stay offended with us.
Jesus said that people will be offended by Him and
by those who follow Him (Matt. 11:6). But even if they
reject us, we do not have the right to reject them. Our
only righteous option is to love them even if they
become enemies to us. "But I say, love your enemies!
Pray for those who persecute you!" (Matt. 5:44).

Though they may choose to break off the relationship, we do not have the same choice. We must love
them when they don't love us. We must serve them
even when they don't appreciate it. And we must continue to honor them above ourselves.

Paul describes our required attitude this way:

> Don't be selfish; don't live to make a good
> impression on others. Be humble, thinking of
> others as better than yourself. Don't think only
> about your own affairs, but be interested in
> others, too, and what they are doing.
>
> Your attitude should be the same that Christ
> Jesus had. Though he was God, he did not
> demand and cling to his rights as God. He
> made himself nothing; he took the humble

position of a slave and appeared in human form. And in human form he obediently humbled himself even further by dying a criminal's death on a cross.

—PHILIPPIANS 2:3–8

THE FEAR OF SEEMING IGNORANT

Remember Tom and his brother, William? Tom was intimidated by his brother's intelligence and education. He feared saying the wrong thing or not being able to answer his brother's questions.

The truth is that none of us have all the answers for all the questions people may ask us. But living by these simple truths will help us deal with this fear.

Avoid arguing about religion with unsaved loved ones.

It is important to avoid religious arguments with our families or relatives. Some will try to debate trivial matters or religious doctrines or traditions. We don't need to get caught trying to defend ourselves or our church. The focus of our discussion must be Jesus. Keep the main thing the main thing! One's personal relationship with Jesus is the main thing—everything else is secondary and pales in significance.

> The Lord's servants must not quarrel but must be kind to everyone. They must be able to teach effectively and be patient with difficult people. They should gently teach those who oppose the truth. Perhaps God will change those people's

hearts, and they will believe the truth. Then they will come to their senses and escape from the Devil's trap. For they have been held captive by him to do whatever he wants.

—2 TIMOTHY 2:24–26

Study God's Word and be ready to witness about what Christ has done in your life.

While Tom did not believe he was William's intellectual equal, he did have the opportunity to know much more about the Scriptures than William. Tom was without excuse if he didn't know what Jesus said about Himself as the Son of God. He should and could know the promises of salvation just by studying the Bible.

Paul's instruction to Timothy is for all believers:

> Study to shew thyself approved unto God, a workman that needeth not to be ashamed, rightly dividing the word of truth. But shun profane and vain babblings: for they will increase unto more ungodliness.
>
> —2 TIMOTHY 2:15–16, KJV

We should also be able to tell others what Jesus has done in our lives. Scripture instructs us, "But sanctify the Lord God in your hearts: and be ready always to give an answer to every man that asketh you a reason of the hope that is in you with meekness and fear" (1 Pet. 3:15, KJV).

Don't be afraid.

The Holy Spirit will put the right words in your mouth. Often I find myself actually listening in amazement to what is coming out of my mouth when I am talking to others about Christ. The Holy Spirit inspires me to say things I had never thought of before. What He guides me in saying is always just what the unbeliever needs to hear. Jesus promises that "the Holy Spirit will teach you what needs to be said even as you are standing there" (Luke 12:12).

A few years ago on a transatlantic flight from Germany back to the States, I spread out my Bible, computer and notepad on my tray table and began to work intensely on a message that I was to preach upon my return. The man sitting next to me eyed my open Bible, made a pronounced frown and downed two drinks in rapid succession before falling sound asleep and snoring loudly.

I continued to work until dinner came. My seatmate stirred and started picking selectively at our typical airplane meal. Between bites, he mumbled his observation, "So you must be a preacher with your Bible, computer and notes. I've no use for preachers."

"Really?" I replied.

"Yeah, all they do is produce guilt and take people's hard-earned money," he mused with more than a slight hint of disgust.

"I hear what you're saying. I am a pastor, but I believe that what people need to hear is the Good News about Jesus, not the bad news about religion."

"So what does your church believe?" he queried.

"Jesus."

"There's got to be more," he snapped.

"My focus is Jesus," I continued. "Discussing anything else simply detracts from the center focus of my faith—Jesus."

Suddenly, he seemed more interested and less hostile. He explained how he had just flown to Germany to buy a new projector for the planetarium he directed in a large, urban area. He proudly told me of his academic credentials, which included a Ph.D. in astronomy. At first I felt intimidated, but I didn't let that get in my way.

As he talked, I realized that Christians had hurt him in the past. He gave a long tirade against the local churches and preachers in his city who had demonstrated against a recent planetarium program that showed the scientific theories about the beginnings of the universe but did not include creationism. The local churches had tried to get government officials to pull the funding for his planetarium—hence his disdain for churches and preachers.

I listened to him through the entrée, dessert and coffee. He finally paused to sigh deeply and ask, "So what do you have good to say about Christians?"

"Christians come in all kinds of packages, but God only comes in one," I responded.

"Sounds like a preacher to me," he commented. "And what package is that?"

"He came in a human package named Jesus. We can know God by knowing His Son, Jesus." Then for the next hour we talked civilly about Jesus—His life, teachings, miracles, death and resurrection. When the plane landed, we were still visiting about Jesus.

No, he didn't make a confession of faith right then and there. But yes, he did listen to the Good News about Jesus. My point? Sharing about Jesus cuts through all the religion, dogma and ecclesiastical blunders from the Crusades and the Inquisition to the fall of present-day televangelists.

Don't fight with family about religion. Focus your conversation on the only One who matters—Jesus, the Christ.

THE FEAR OF BEING SHAMED

We may fear being put to shame—or even bringing shame to Christ—when we share the gospel. While we may fear being shamed and losing face or having our reputation smeared, the fact is that we have already confessed our shame and lost our reputation. We are of no reputation—just like Christ: "But made Himself of no reputation, taking the form of a bond-servant, and coming in the likeness of men" (Phil. 2:7, NKJV).

Years ago, a popular Christian youth speaker, Ken Davis, would say to youth, "As a Christian, you have nothing to fear, nothing to lose and nothing to hide." So when the wall of fear threatens to block your witness, remember these important insights:

You have nothing to fear.

What can mere humans do to you when God is on

your side? You have nothing to fear from your loved ones. There is nothing they can do to harm or hurt you. The Bible assures you:

> What can we say about such wonderful things as these? If God is for us, who can ever be against us? Since God did not spare even his own Son but gave him up for us all, won't God, who gave us Christ, also give us everything else?
> Who dares accuse us whom God has chosen for his own? Will God? No! He is the one who has given us right standing with himself. Who then will condemn us? Will Christ Jesus? No, for he is the one who died for us and was raised to life for us and is sitting at the place of highest honor next to God, pleading for us.
>
> —ROMANS 8:31–34

You have nothing to lose.

You have already lost your life. You have already been crucified with Christ. Your body is already a living sacrifice. And you have surrendered all your possessions and rights to Christ. You are simply a steward of His boundless resources. Jesus says, "Whoever clings to this life will lose it, and whoever loses this life will save it" (Luke 17:33). You have nothing to lose when you share Jesus with a family member, and everything to gain—including a brother or sister in Christ for eternity!

You have nothing to hide.

Your sins have already been confessed and forgiven. Though your lost family members may know about your rotten past—and may condemn you for it—you have already repented of everything and been forgiven by Christ. When you are accused of past sins, you can simply say, "That's true. I admit it. But I have quit doing that. I am forgiven of my past sin by Jesus Christ. I ask you to forgive me, too. Will you?"

You have nothing to be ashamed of. You can say with Paul:

> For I am not ashamed of this Good News about Christ. It is the power of God at work, saving everyone who believes—Jews first and also Gentiles. This Good News tells us how God makes us right in his sight. This is accomplished from start to finish by faith. As the Scriptures say, "It is through faith that a righteous person has life."
>
> —ROMANS 1:16–17

TEAR DOWN THE WALL

I once heard a Bible teacher claim that Scripture says "fear not" in its various grammatical forms over 365 times. After checking a concordance, I don't doubt his assertion. He also said that one reason Scripture talks so much about fear is because we need daily assurance that we have nothing to fear from either God or man.

Take to heart just a few of God's promises assuring us that we have nothing to fear:

> Be strong and of a good courage, fear not, nor be afraid of them: for the LORD thy God, he it is that doth go with thee; he will not fail thee, nor forsake thee.
>
> —DEUTERONOMY 31:6, KJV

> Say to them that are of a fearful heart, Be strong, fear not: behold, your God will come with vengeance, even God with a recompense; he will come and save you.
>
> —ISAIAH 35:4, KJV

> But when Jesus heard it, he answered him, saying, Fear not: believe only, and she shall be made whole.
>
> —LUKE 8:50, KJV

> Fear not, little flock; for it is your Father's good pleasure to give you the kingdom.
>
> —LUKE 12:32, KJV

> And when I saw him, I fell at his feet as dead. And he laid his right hand upon me, saying unto me, Fear not; I am the first and the last: I am he that liveth, and was dead; and, behold, I am alive for evermore, Amen; and have the keys of hell and of death.
>
> —REVELATION 1:17–18, KJV

Take God at His Word and fear not. Allow God to be your sure defense; trust Him to give you the right words to say and the right things to do as you live for Jesus in front of your lost family members. Make the decision now that you will not let fear silence your witness. God's power and strength will back you up, because "God hath not given us the spirit of fear; but of power, and of love, and of a sound mind" (2 Tim. 1:7, KJV).

Practical steps

- Look up the promises in Scripture dealing with fear. Begin to trust God at His Word to remove your every fear.
- Bind the spirit of fear in prayer and bind yourself to the will of God before sharing about Jesus with a family member. Loose the fruits of God's Spirit in your life so that your witness will reflect His fruit. "But the fruit of the Spirit is love, joy, peace, longsuffering, gentleness, goodness, faith, meekness, temperance: against such there is no law" (Gal. 5:22–23, KJV).
- Memorize key scripture passages to share with family members who are lost. Sharing God's Word when you witness is sometimes more effective than giving opinions or explaining personal doctrines. It's also effective to paraphrase these scriptures into your own words. When the Holy Spirit gives you the right words to say, He often uses Scripture that is already in you. Start with memorizing these passages: John 1:12;

John 3:16; John 10:28; Acts 2:38; Romans 3:23; Romans 5:1–2; Romans 5:6–10; Romans 10:9, 13; 1 John 5:11–13.
• Find another believer who will help you role-play a conversation with your lost family member. Describe to your believing friend how your family member normally reacts when you try to share the gospel or talk about Jesus. As you role-play with your friend, he or she can help you discover ways to witness that are loving yet bold.

You might also do an exercise with your believing friend that will help you identify what might be hindering you. Begin by saying, "I believe in God." Then have your believing friend ask, "Why?" Respond with a sentence, to which your friend will again ask, "Why?" Continue this dialogue until you have exhausted all your answers. Now go through the same exercise beginning with the statement, "I believe in Jesus." Completing both of these dialogues will help you talk through your faith and testimony. Accept feedback from your believing friend on how you came across—loving, frustrated, bold, assertive, aggressive, kind or caring.

Such role-playing will help you develop an effective witness for Christ with family members and will build confidence while overcoming the wall of fear. Trust this promise from God:"Do not throw away this confident trust in the Lord, no matter what happens. Remember the great reward it brings you!" (Heb. 10:35). Confidently trust God's Spirit to teach you what to say, how to react and how to overcome fear in witnessing to your family.

Pray

Trust God's power to destroy the wall of fear in your life. Consider praying this:

> *Lord Jesus, I trust You at Your Word, which tells me to "fear not." I believe that through Your mighty power I have nothing to fear, nothing to hide and nothing to lose. I come against the spirit of fear as I witness to my lost family members. I pray for Your love, Your power and a sound mind to guide me as I share about You with each person in my family. I now replace the wall of fear with Your protection and presence. Amen.*

Reach out

You can dismantle the wall of fear and reach out to your lost loved one by:

- Choosing scriptures to share that best fit the lifestyle of your family member.
- Speaking aloud some of the "fear not" promises from Scripture whenever you feel fearful about sharing your faith.
- Sharing about your wall of fear with a believing friend or your pastor. Pray in agreement with them that the wall of fear will be destroyed.
- Remembering to focus on Jesus when sharing with a lost loved one. Don't allow yourself to be

distracted by arguments, confusing doctrines or traditions. Keep the main thing the main thing. Jesus is the main thing you want to share with a lost family member.

- Going through the Gospel of John and reading all the "I AM" passages about Jesus. Learn who Jesus is through His self-revelation and share that with those who are lost. Here is a start:

John 6:35 — I AM the bread of life.

John 7:37 — I AM living water.

John 8:12 — I AM the light of the world.

John 8:58 — I AM.

John 10:7, 9 — I AM the door.

John 10:11, 14 — I AM the good shepherd.

John 11:25 — I AM the resurrection and the life.

John 14:6 — I AM the way, the truth and the life.

John 15:1, 5 — I AM the true vine.

Do you wish your family would get saved? Go beyond your fear. Know that their salvation is eternally more important than the possibility that they might reject you. Secure in Jesus, you have nothing to fear, nothing to lose and nothing to hide from your family. Let them see the new creation Jesus has made of you. Fear not!

CHAPTER 6

THE WALLS OF RELIGIOUS ARROGANCE, BUSYNESS AND LOVE GROWING COLD

A nita worked with my wife years ago in nursing. As a charge nurse, she had significant responsibilities and influence over a number of hospital personnel and patients. And everyone in her sphere of influence knew that she professed to be saved! In fact, rarely did a day go by when Anita didn't brashly intrude into a patient's or colleague's privacy with her insistence that that person needed Jesus. Her judgmental and critical remarks left those around her dreading any reference to Jesus from her or anyone else.

Furthermore, her life was a living testimony to a mess. Her children were constantly having problems, and her marriage was on the rocks—yet everything was an attack of the enemy. Almost everyone else was on the road to hell except her. When things were going rather smoothly for her, everything was "Praise the Lord" and "Thank You, Jesus." But within minutes her mood could change from sunny skies to torrential storms.

Simply put, Anita's family and friends were repulsed by her wall of religious arrogance flaunted in the name of Jesus. Anita's religion was a crutch that she used to manipulate, blame and control others because her life was out of control. The very things for which she judged others, she was guilty of in varying degrees.

THE WALL OF RELIGIOUS ARROGANCE

As we discussed earlier, knowing Jesus makes us servants, not masters. Knowing the sin from which we have been delivered gives us a deeper love for others in sin. Because Jesus in His great mercy saved me, a sinner, I know He will save others—no matter how terrible their sin. I have no right to judge them, only to love them and share Jesus with them.

The arrogant, religious leaders of Jesus' day condemned those who did not know or follow religious law and tradition the way they did. Instead of commending their religious righteousness, Jesus said:

How terrible it will be for you teachers of religious law and you Pharisees. Hypocrites! For you

> won't let others enter the Kingdom of Heaven,
> and you won't go in yourselves. Yes, how terrible
> it will be for you teachers of religious law and
> you Pharisees. For you cross land and sea to
> make one convert, and then you turn him into
> twice the son of hell as you yourselves are.
> —MATTHEW 23:13–15

You and I are not better than the unsaved. We have only been broken, repentant, forgiven and set free. An attitude of religious arrogance serves only to drive family and friends away from Jesus. Instead, we want to drive them to their knees in repentance through showing His kindness and love.

A business friend of mine years ago commented that sometimes relationship is more important than being right. Just because we are right about Christ and have been made righteous in Him doesn't give us the right to judge a family member and strain that relationship. Instead of spiritual arrogance, we need to show kindness and humility.

Replacing arrogance with kindness and humility

As editor of *Ministries Today,* a magazine for church leaders, I get to know many wonderful spiritual leaders. I highly value the wisdom of one of our columnists, Pastor Ted Haggard of New Life Church in Colorado Springs, Colorado. Consider his comments:

> The reputation of Christianity is changing in
> America. Not long ago, the phrase "good

Christian" was used to describe people who were virtuous, trustworthy, kind, fair and giving. When someone had a Christian as a landlord, lawyer or laborer, they trusted them to be honest, humble and helpful. Kindness was assumed. Humility was a given.

Today, too many Christians, including leaders, have lost that reputation. In many people's opinion of Christians, kindness and humility have been replaced with self-promotion, arrogance and self-indulgence.

I don't know if my grandparents were born again or not, but I do know that they stayed married and faithful to one another, raised their children, attended and participated in church regularly and read their Bibles daily. They never ate a meal without thanking God. They helped their neighbors, gave to the poor and loved the Lord with all of their hearts. They never cussed, drank, cheated or stole anything. My grandparents were kind—virtues that are too often lacking in today's church. They cared for the sick in the community and coached struggling families. They never accepted a government handout or benefit—that would have been considered shameful.

I doubt that they ever raised their hands in church, heard a personal prophecy or were slain in the Spirit, but somehow they knew the will of God. And certainly their community trusted them, honored them and valued their participation. They were loved and appreciated. They were "good Christian people." I'm not advocating going back to where they were, but I do believe we have much to learn from our elders.

It interests me that they believed that humility and kindness are Christian virtues. I remember watching my grandmother's face subtly wince one time as she listened to a man promoting himself. I asked her afterward what she thought of the man. She gently explained that he was a good man, but that we should never praise or promote ourselves. Her response wasn't judgmental or critical, but she did communicate that we as a family didn't believe that it was honorable to praise ourselves. And she really believed that.

She and others like her were the ones who were easily elected to school boards, city councils and county commissions. Non-Christians trusted people like our grandparents. Even when they didn't agree with them, they liked them, trusted them and knew that the world was a better place because of them.

Not true today. Today, Christianity is associated with hating homosexuals, not appreciating civil liberties, and self-exaltation. And it's no wonder. Too many of our leaders unnecessarily fly in private airplanes, are ushered into back rooms before and after ministry so they won't be exposed to "common" people, and spend too much time on the platform telling people that to get the benefits of Jesus' love they need to give more money or buy their products.

The public can't figure us out. We need to help them—by earning back the strong reputation that previous generations established. Paul simply had it right: "Instead, be kind to each other, tenderhearted, forgiving one another, just as God through Christ has forgiven you" (Eph. 4:32).

I believe we would see less divorce in our Spirit-filled churches if husbands and wives would simply be kind to each other. We would probably see less teenage rebellion, fewer church fights in church business meetings and greater impact of the gospel on our cities if we practiced kindness with humility. In fact, being Spirit-filled means to produce the fruit of kindness. Could it be that meanness in the body is a lack of the Spirit moving in our midst? Could it be that our arrogance and lack of humility is the very thing that hinders revival?

Simply put, we need a revival of values: a touch of kindness and a pinch of humility.[1]

Do our unsaved family members know us as kind, honest, humble and trustworthy? Are they seeing the fruit of the Spirit in our lives? Our relationship with them should be more important than being right all the time.

Replacing religious language

One of the most subtle ways we put up the wall of religious arrogance is through the use of religious language. We use terms and clichés that unsaved people don't understand and certainly don't appreciate.

In our evangelism training, we show people how to witness using nonreligious language. Instead of asking a lost loved one, "Are you saved or born again?" you might ask, "Do you have a relationship with God or Jesus?" Christians may call a sin a "transgression." To the unsaved, sin might be better addressed as a "moral failure" or "breaking God's law." In other words, we need to find new words to better communicate these spiritual concepts to unsaved family members.

Look at the list of religious terms below. Write every word you can think of that you could use instead of the religious term. Avoid spiritual or theological words.

Saved _____

Church _____

Sin _____

Savior _____

Lord _____

Christ _____

Holy Spirit _____

Justification _____

Praise the Lord _____

Sanctification _____

Redemption _____

Baptism _____

Repentance _____

Heavenly Father _____

Try to share about Jesus with your unsaved family members using terms they can understand instead of the "Christianese" that believers use among themselves.

THE WALL OF BUSYNESS

I must confess that I am writing to myself as I pen these words. Ministry, writing, editing, family and life's nitty-gritty details keep me very busy. What about you? Do you find yourself rushing through days and weeks not even being able to remember what you did yesterday or the day before? Is it difficult to find time for your immediate family, much less your aunts, uncles, cousins and other relatives?

The wall of busyness means that the gospel doesn't get shared with lost loved ones because we are too busy to:

- Pray regularly, even daily, for our lost family members.
- Call them on the phone and listen to what's important in their lives.

- Go by for visits.
- Send them notes, letters, faxes or e-mails.
- Give them gifts that could introduce them to Christ, such as Bibles or good Christian inspirational books or novels.

Busyness is the devil's scheme to keep us from the important things of God. Keeping up with the urgent is Satan's way of making us think we are accomplishing much when, in truth, nothing eternal is happening through what we are doing. Busyness is Lucifer's way of sending darkness to a relationship that needs the light of time, sharing and laughter. Are you too busy?

We may feel uncomfortable around certain lost family members. I know it's more fun to be with family and friends who think like us and who share the same eternal destination we do. But the issue here isn't fun—it's salvation! It is better to be uncomfortable and build relationships that lead to people getting saved than to be comfortable and busily miss the truth that they are lost and going to hell.

So if you find yourself too busy, put this book down immediately and contact your loved one. Rebuild broken family relationships. Set your comfort zone aside and go for what's important in life—getting your family saved!

THE WALL OF LOVE GROWING COLD

Jesus warned that in the last days, "sin will be rampant

everywhere, and the love of many will grow cold" (Matt. 24:12). Not sharing Jesus with lost family members simply reveals a lack of love for them.

Over the years I have found myself trying to demonstrate my love for my lost family members in many different ways. But as they continued to rebuff my attempts to share Jesus, I slowly grew indifferent. I would still send birthday cards or Christmas gifts, but the zeal to share Jesus waned. I stopped trying to talk to them about my faith.

Then I would feel guilty and commence a new barrage of innovative ways to reach out to them. Occasionally something I tried would work. But often, my reaching out was rebuffed, and again I grew discouraged. Nonetheless, I came to understand that not sharing Jesus with them was a problem of *my* heart. I was waxing cold of heart toward them. If I truly loved them, I would keep sharing Jesus with them!

One mark of genuine love for others is wanting the best for them. And certainly the best for lost loved ones is their having personal, eternal relationships with Jesus Christ. When we truly love our family members, we will faithfully reach out to them in whatever way we can to lead them to Jesus. Sharing Jesus with someone who is lost is true love! LOVE IS A DECISION

Tear Down the Walls

Getting religious arrogance and busyness out of our lives are probably goals that we already have. And who wants their love for others to grow cold? These walls in us need to come down—and they can!

Practical steps

We can take some practical steps that will tear down each of the following walls.

Tearing down the wall of *religious arrogance* means that we must:

- Humble ourselves.
- Repent of self-righteousness and pride.
- Focus on right relationships instead of having to be right all the time.
- Listen to others instead of preaching at them.

Tearing down the wall of *busyness* involves:

- Scheduling time to be with lost family members.
- Taking time to write, fax or e-mail lost loved ones.
- Deciding that the salvation of lost loved ones is an important priority in our lives and then taking time for it.
- Going beyond our comfort zones to witness— even to the point of being uncomfortable.

Tearing down the wall of *love growing cold* will require us to:

- Pray for zeal in witnessing to our family.
- Love our family even when they don't love us in return.

- Believe that the greatest gift of love we can give a family member is knowing Jesus.

Pray

We help tear down these walls by praying:

Lord Jesus, break my pride and humble me. Show me ways I can be kind to my family members. Help me make spending time with family a priority. Show me ways to share You with my family even when it's not comfortable. Lord, increase my fervor, zeal and love for my family so that my greatest joy will be in seeing them saved. Amen.

Reach out

Once the walls of religious arrogance, busyness and love growing cold have begun to come down, you might reach out to your lost loved one by:

- Making time for them a priority in your schedule.
- Writing, faxing and e-mailing them.
- Avoiding the use of religious terms that don't communicate clearly to them.
- Replacing judging them with being kind to them and finding ways to demonstrate kindness in the little things of life.
- Loving them with words that affirm and edify and caring for them, particularly at times of need, such as sickness, financial difficulty and relational stress.

It's not only important to tear down all the walls we have discussed, but it's also just as important to keep the walls down. Prayer, staying in the Word, being led by the Holy Spirit, staying accountable to other believers and keeping your family's salvation as a prime priority in your life will help you keep the walls down!

SECTION II

WHAT'S IN THEM THAT'S KEEPING JESUS OUT?

Jim started sharing with his younger brother, Alan, the exciting new things the Lord was doing in his life. The more Jim shared, the more agitated Alan became. Jim was seven years older than Alan and had been gone from home a long time. When he left, Alan had been a strong believer. What Jim didn't realize, however, was that Alan had experienced a severe jolt to his faith in high school.

Alan had somehow been labeled as the family's black sheep. Jim had achieved high grades in high school and had gone off to college. Alan, however, had struggled scholastically and went to vocational school to learn a trade.

Their parents constantly bragged on Jim and constantly used his example when talking to Alan. When Alan had brought home poor grades, his parents would cajole, "Why can't you get the grades that Jim got? You have the same potential. You're just lazy."

At times Alan's attitude and rebellion put him at odds with his family and the law. His long hair and baggy attire also brought some rejection at the church youth group. However, Alan did enjoy going—especially when Angie, the daughter of one of the deacons, was there. But Angie's parents did not like Alan's attitude or taste in fashions, and they labeled him a rebel and a pagan, forbidding her to see him.

The truth was that Alan did love the Lord but was struggling with a multitude of questions about the church. The way Angie's parents treated Alan pushed him away not only from the church but also from God. Alan felt that if Christians couldn't love him unconditionally the way Christ did, then he had no use for the church. The more Angie's parents rejected him, the deeper Alan's hurt grew until it became a festering wound. Then a root of bitterness sprang up within him.

The unhealed wound lingered into Alan's adult life. He hadn't returned to church and had no interest at all in faith. Since Jim hadn't been around during his brother's high school years, he was completely blindsided when Alan raged at him, "You can take your religion and Jesus talk and shove it. I want nothing to do with any of it. And don't bring it up again in the future."

Jim now knew the wall of hurt in Alan that kept him from Jesus. His challenge became ministering to Alan to help him heal from the hurt. At the same time, Jim could gently relay the Good News of Jesus Christ. A tough process lay ahead, but guided by the Holy Spirit, Jim would be able to approach his brother wisely with the love of Christ.

WALLS IN OTHERS

After tearing down the walls in us that keep Jesus from our lost family members, here's the question we must now ask: What walls in them are keeping them from receiving Jesus? Once we know that, we can ask ourselves:

- How can I be an instrument of God in disman tling the walls?
- What words are needed?
- What action will best circumvent the walls so that I can share without being shut off?
- How should I pray?
- How long should I try?

In the coming chapters you will learn how to discern the walls in your lost loved ones that keep Jesus out. You will also discover practical ways to reach them with the gospel. Now that your walls are down, it's time to help your lost family get saved by dismantling theirs.

CHAPTER 7

THE WALL
OF SELF

Joan was happily married to a kind, reliable man, and they had three school-age children. Her family was what most people would call ideal, but in reality, her household was anything but. You see, Joan believed that her family's world revolved around her. Holidays were celebrated her way, or else she ranted and raved until everyone was beaten down and she got her way. Joan knew that her every opinion was right, and she didn't acknowledge her children's ideas as even worth considering if they differed from hers. Joan continually talked about herself—her aches and pains, her problems, her needs and her ideas. And worst of all, Joan didn't have a clue that she was so self-centered.

As a result of her wall of self, she effectively isolated herself from her family. And they gladly found ways to avoid her. Of course, their actions reinforced to her that she was the victim. After all, her only flaw was being right, and her family should be glad they had someone so clever to rely on.

One day Joan was on her way to the store to pick up a missing ingredient for a cookie recipe when she accidentally ran a stop sign and ran into a minivan. Joan was the only one injured, and a helicopter rushed her to the triage unit at a local hospital. After a three-hour surgery, doctors pronounced her stable—all internal injuries were repaired.

What wasn't repaired, though, was Joan's spiritual heart. That's when Joan's single sister, Sylvia, decided to reach out to her and share the gospel. Joan wasn't interested in anything Sylvia had to say, so Sylvia decided to *show* her God's love. As Joan recuperated in the hospital, Sylvia took care of Joan's family, making meals for them as well. Then she spent evenings with Joan in the hospital when Joan's husband arrived home and took over watching the children.

Those evening hours began to soften Joan's wall of selfishness. She was forced to face the fact that she had been at fault in this accident. That helped her see other ways she was at fault. Slowly the bricks of self-centeredness were removed. Sylvia showed God's love by not judging Joan, but instead by helping her

through the painful realizations. Joan's heart soft-
ened, and Sylvia was able to lead her sister to Christ.

SIN STARTS IN SELF

Every wall that keeps someone from Christ is constructed from the raw material of sin. And at the core
of sin is self.

Self is a very powerful force in the life of a person. It
is at the heart of the survival instinct, which keeps us
alive in times of danger. That is a good thing, but self
seeks preservation at all cost. When not kept in rein
by a moral character and by God, self can destroy us
and others.

The desire to run our own lives and to control
our own destinies springs from selfishness or self-
centeredness—and it gets in the way of our
relationship with God. We can fall into the same trap
Adam and Eve did when they ate of the fruit of the
serpent's temptation: "God knows that your eyes will
be opened when you eat it. You will become just like
God, knowing everything, both good and evil" (Gen.
3:5).

Keith Miller provides an excellent overview of the
relationship between self-centeredness and sin in *Sin:
Overcoming the Ultimate Deadly Addiction.* Keith says
that as an addiction, sin prompts us to deny that we
have problems, needs or addictions:

> Our sin offers us a seemingly perfect way out of
> a painful dilemma. Through a process called

denial we can rationalize and trick ourselves
into thinking we aren't exactly transgressing our
values, or that, if we are, it is actually for the
good of the person we are hurting....

The true crime is self-centeredness, emotional desertion and abuse of others, about
which we are in denial.[1]

The wall of self becomes a fortress of selfishness or
self-centeredness that keeps us in denial that anything
is wrong with us or that we have any problems. We
see ourselves as good people no matter how many
people we may be hurting—including ourselves. We
reason that someone else is always to blame for
broken relationships—not us.

Sin protects self above all else. Preservation of
one's feelings, thoughts, freedom and actions
become the primary drive in the selfish person. So
sharing about the ultimate servant, the Selfless One,
with self-centered people can be threatening to them.
If there is a selfless way to live, they don't want to hear
about it, much less surrender to it.

DISCERNING THE WALL OF SELF-CENTEREDNESS

Discerning a selfish or self-centered person requires
little effort. Action, attitudes and prideful talk usually
mark the person full of self. These warning signs can
be easily recognized:

- Seeking to be promoted while never promoting
  others

- Talking endlessly about self but rarely listening
- Always wanting to know, "What's in it for me?"
- Requiring lots of attention
- Hurting easily when not noticed or recognized in ways they deem appropriate
- Cruising down the road of life, leaving dead or dying relationships in their wake, but never being aware of the hurt they've inflicted
- Wanting positions of leadership instead of humbly serving
- Tearing others down or gossiping so that they can look good in comparison
- Being defensive when feeling threatened
- Denying making even the smallest mistakes

THE BRICKS OF PRIDE

The basic material out of which the wall of self is constructed is pride. But the manifestations of pride can appear in many different forms. In addition to selfishness, let's explore a few other bricks of pride that are used in building the wall of self.

Brick #1: Self-gratification

Lost people consumed with self-gratification believe that anything that pleases or gratifies their senses will bring happiness. They love things and use people instead of using things and loving people. In Luke 12 Jesus shows us that self-gratification became the hallmark of the rich fool's life:

Then he said, "Beware! Don't be greedy for what you don't have. Real life is not measured by how much we own."

And he gave an illustration: "A rich man had a fertile farm that produced fine crops. In fact, his barns were full to overflowing. So he said, 'I know! I'll tear down my barns and build bigger ones. Then I'll have room enough to store everything. And I'll sit back and say to myself, My friend, you have enough stored away for years to come. Now take it easy! Eat, drink, and be merry!'

"But God said to him, 'You fool! You will die this very night. Then who will get it all?'

"Yes, a person is a fool to store up earthly wealth but not have a rich relationship with God."

—LUKE 12:15–21

When lost family members build their walls of self with the bricks of self-gratification, they often display some of these attitudes or actions:

- Acquiring instead of giving
- Becoming owners instead of stewards
- Being motivated by greed, not generosity
- Never having or owning enough
- Working harder to earn more and buy more
- Emphasizing materialism while neglecting spirituality
- Measuring worth in temporal, not eternal, standards

- Believing the end justifies the means when acquiring wealth
- Valuing people for their possessions, not for their character and values
- Tolerating immorality because it feels good

Brick #2: Self-Degradation

Believe it or not, some people take pride in being victims. They receive a feeling of worth and attention by flaunting their problems and crises. They maintain a constant state of self-degradation so that others will feel sorry for them. By doing so, they focus attention on themselves, and they have a great need for attention.

Unsaved family members wallowing in the muck of self-pity often blame everyone else for their problems. They find excuse after excuse for why they cannot get to Jesus—the One who can save, heal and deliver them from their wretched state.

The biblical narrative that depicts this state of self-degradation is found in John 5:

> One of the men lying there had been sick for thirty-eight years. When Jesus saw him and knew how long he had been ill, he asked him, "Would you like to get well?"
>
> "I can't, sir," the sick man said, "for I have no one to help me into the pool when the water is stirred up. While I am trying to get there, someone else always gets in ahead of me."
>
> Jesus told him, "Stand up, pick up your

sleeping mat, and walk!"
Instantly, the man was healed! He rolled up
the mat and began walking!

—JOHN 5:5–9

Because he had been focused on his illness for thirty-eight years, this paralytic couldn't see beyond his sickness to his healing. He continually blamed others for his state and thus immersed himself daily—not in the pool of God's healing but in the pool of self-pity.

When lost family members build their walls of self with the bricks of self-degradation, they typically display some of these attitudes or actions:

- Preferring sickness over health
- Blaming others for their plights
- Using their problems to attract the attention of others
- Desiring sympathy more than empathy
- Seeking pity rather than help or healing
- Believing that they can never change
- Feeling that they are limited and bound by their past
- Maintaining the status quo instead of learning how to regenerate and grow

Brick #3: Self-Actualization

What's wrong with self-actualization? you may ask. To begin with, human potential—not our destiny in God—is the main ingredient of the brick of self-actualization. Seeking self-actualization leads lost

106

family members to take every new self-help seminar and read every possible how-to book on self-improvement. They block out the gospel's message that "all have sinned; all fall short of God's glorious standard" (Rom. 3:23). All they hunger for is to know how to get better and better—by themselves. They typify the observation of Paul, "Always learning and never able to come to the knowledge of the truth" (2 Tim. 3:7, NKJV).

Psychotherapists such as Abraham Maslow and Carl Rogers offer lost people unfounded optimism about their potential. Person-centered therapy tends to be naively and romantically optimistic, often claiming an unlimited potential for growth from within. This can be less than helpful to those whose hurt and pain reflect a greater variety of biological, psychological or socio-cultural causes than merely "blocks to their self-actualization."

Salvation might be palatable to those seeking self-actualization if only they could earn or achieve it. Such lost loved ones hemmed in by their walls of self are like the young man described in Matthew 19:

> Someone came to Jesus with this question: "Teacher, what good things must I do to have eternal life?"
>
> "Why ask me about what is good?" Jesus replied. "Only God is good. But to answer your question, you can receive eternal life if you keep the commandments."
>
> "Which ones?" the man asked.

And Jesus replied: "'Do not murder. Do not commit adultery. Do not steal. Do not testify falsely. Honor your father and mother. Love your neighbor as yourself.'"

"I've obeyed all these commandments," the young man replied. "What else must I do?"

Jesus told him, "If you want to be perfect, go and sell all you have and give the money to the poor, and you will have treasure in heaven. Then come, follow me." But when the young man heard this, he went sadly away because he had many possessions.

—Matthew 19:16–22

This young man's identify was anchored in his ability to do good and possess much. His need to achieve far exceeded his desire to be set free and saved. For him, the forbidden fruit of the tree of the knowledge of good and evil was the knowledge of good. Good had replaced God. Good he could achieve. But since salvation can never be earned, he bypassed the gift of eternal life.

God saved you by his special favor when you believed. And you can't take credit for this; it is a gift from God. Salvation is not a reward for the good things we have done, so none of us can boast about it.

—Ephesians 2:8–9

Those family members building their wall of self out of the bricks of self-actualization will often display these attitudes and actions:

- Pursuing self-help rather than God's help
- Always learning new ways to become better persons
- Prizing human knowledge over wisdom and revelation
- Feeling as though they don't need salvation because they are already good people
- Being proud of their achievements
- Working hard to gain personal satisfaction and recognition from others
- Seeing effort and accomplishment as more important than trusting and receiving from God or others

KEYS TO BREAKING THROUGH THE WALL OF SELF

As mentioned earlier, sin relies heavily on denial. Walls remain up as long as the lost person is deceived into believing lies and denying truth. The only truth is Jesus Christ—the way, the truth and the life. One way to approach a lost family member blinded by denial is by living the truth of God's Word.

Let's look at some keys to penetrating the wall of self.

Key 1: Don't be greedy.

Greed, materialism and the pursuit of worldly possessions mark people surrounded by walls of self-gratification. They tend to surround themselves with like-minded people. That way, the counsel and advice they receive mostly focuses on how to acquire more and get richer.

Believers who are still influenced by the stronghold of greed will not have any power to reach the self-oriented lost. Sinners immediately discern when a believer is motivated by greed. That means that greed in our lives will simply harden greedy family members against the gospel.

We are called to live selfless, simple and humble lives. Instead of being jealous of the possessions of selfish family members, we need to exemplify selfless living.

Give praise and honor to Christ for all you have. The answer is being content. Let your unsaved family members hear you give praise and honor to Christ for whatever you have—a lot or a little. Share with them how God—not your career, education, job, inheritance or investments—is your source. When they talk about their riches, share about your riches in Christ.

> You know how full of love and kindness our Lord Jesus Christ was. Though he was very rich, yet for your sakes he became poor, so that by his poverty he could make you rich.
>
> —2 CORINTHIANS 8:9

Don't compete with or compare yourself to greedy, unsaved family members. Your message is not, "My God is richer than your god. He makes me wealthier than you." Paul writes, "Be sure to do what you should, for then you will enjoy the personal satisfaction of having done your work well, and you won't need to compare yourself to anyone else" (Gal. 6:4). The good news you have to share is, "And this same God who takes care of me will supply all your needs from his glorious riches, which have been given to us in Christ Jesus" (Phil. 4:19).

Refuse to condemn them for their riches. Jesus reminded us that we are like true children of our Father in heaven when we are good to everyone. "For he gives his sunlight to both the evil and the good, and he sends rain on the just and on the unjust, too" (Matt. 5:45). Instead of condemning them for their riches, show them you are content with what you have—and that your possessions are not the basis for your happiness. For those who selfishly seek riches, this is the good news that shatters their wall of greed. Help them understand that you see Christ as the greatest treasure of all:

> I love all who love me. Those who search for me will surely find me. Unending riches, honor, wealth, and justice are mine to distribute. My gifts are better than the purest gold, my wages better than sterling silver! I walk in righteousness, in paths of justice. Those who love me inherit wealth, for I fill their treasuries.
>
> —PROVERBS 8:17–21

Key 2: Don't pity those caught in self-degradation.

Jesus never pitied the sick in body, soul or spirit. He simply offered them the good news. Jesus simply asked the man at the pool of Bethesda, "Would you like to get well?" Yes, he had been sick for years. Yes, others had not helped him into the pool. Yes, life was hard and full of pain and misery. But Jesus reached out with the good news of saving wholeness. He told the man he could walk, and the man responded to the good news in faith.

Stop having pity parties with your lost loved ones. Instead, share the Jesus who saves, heals and delivers. Too often we find ourselves playing the mind game of "Ain't it awful!" We actually give sympathy and even encouragement to the self-degradation of the lost by agreeing with them about their tragic situations. The good news of Jesus that penetrates the wall of self-degradation is this: God is good. Jesus will empower you to step out of your misery and into greatness. You don't have to live life as a cripple—physically, emotionally or spiritually. By faith in Jesus, you can stand up, move on and live abundantly.

Offer hope instead of sympathy. Sympathy agrees with people building the wall of self-degradation. Hope offers an answer on the other side of the wall, beyond the present circumstance. The best gift you can give a lost family member is hope, not sympathy.

Help them see what they can do. People trapped behind the wall of self-degradation often believe they are helpless. They choose to remain victims, seeing themselves as powerless—hopelessly trapped in their problems and circumstances. Jesus offered healing to the paralytic, but the man had to do something. He had to exercise his faith by standing up, picking up his mat and walking.

Tell your lost loved ones that there is something they can do to move beyond the wall of self-degradation. They can trust that Jesus loves them and that He sees them as victors, not victims. He proclaims that they can get up and get on with their lives through His saving power.

Key 3: Point out what's really good.

The wall of self-actualization focuses the unsaved person's attention on personal goodness instead of God. We are instructed to set our eyes on God, not on good.

> I will praise your mighty deeds, O Sovereign
> LORD.
> I will tell everyone that you alone are just and
> good.
> O God, you have taught me from my earliest
> childhood,
> and I have constantly told others about the
> wonderful things you do.
> —PSALM 71:16–17

Jesus moved the rich young man's attention from his own goodness to God who is good. Jesus also directed the young man to follow Him instead of running after the riches of this world.

When sharing Jesus with lost loved ones, we have the choice of focusing on their sin or on God's good. Instead of discrediting the young man's goodness, Jesus simply pointed him in the direction of God's good. Instead of pointing out our loved one's sins, we can affirm the good that is in their lives. Then they may listen when we point beyond them to a life that goes beyond good to God. *Yes, you have done many good things in life. But there is a better way to live. In fact, the best way to live, the highest life to live is following Jesus.*

PRAYING FOR YOUR LOST LOVED ONES

The bondages of sin can be broken by the love of God in Christ. He changes stony, hardened hearts into new, obedient hearts.

> And I will give you a new heart with new and right desires, and I will put a new spirit in you. I will take out your stony heart of sin and give you a new, obedient heart.
> —EZEKIEL 36:26

To see breakthroughs in the stony walls of self, we need to pray:

> *Lord, help me to crucify self that I might be self-less, loving and humble as I relate to others. Keep me focused on You instead of on me. Help me to look beyond the selfishness of my lost loved ones and to serve them the same way You serve. Empower me to see them with Your eyes instead of my own. Fill me with Your love for them. Amen.*

Praying through the wall of self-gratification

Help me, Lord, not to compare myself with my lost loved ones or what I have with what they have. Keep all jealousy out of my heart. Teach me that You are my source so that I can show them that in You all needs are met. Help me to be content with what I have. Amen.

Praying through the wall of self-degradation

Lord, give me Your heart for my lost family members. I desire to value and love them the way You do. Give me compassion instead of sympathy or pity for them. Help me reach out and inspire them to trust You for victory in all of life's circumstances. Amen.

Praying through the wall of self-actualization

Jesus, I know that all my future potential and possibilities lie in You. Give me a vision of who I am in You. Then teach me how to impart that vision to others. Shine through me, Lord Jesus, so that my family may see that to be fully human is to be completely surrendered to the Son of Man. Amen.

Praying for salvation of lost loved ones

Finally, daily pray for the salvation of your lost loved ones using Galatians 2:20. Pray that they tear down the wall of self. That happens when they (like us) crucify self and live in Christ. Pray this, inserting the names of your unsaved family members:

Lord Jesus, I pray that _____ no longer lives, but that You, Christ, lives in _____. Holy Spirit, I ask You to lead _____ to a saving knowledge of Jesus Christ. Heavenly Father, I pray that the life _____ lives in _____'s earthly body will be lived by trusting in You, who loves _____ and gave Yourself for _____. I pray in the power and authority of Jesus' name, amen.

If the wall of self is not the one keeping your loved ones in bondage, then perhaps the wall of guilt and shame is. At times, our lost loved ones may feel so guilty because of past sins that they cannot accept that God truly loves and accepts them. It's time to overcome that wall with God's love.

CHAPTER 8

THE WALL OF
GUILT AND SHAME

~)

Gud could never forgive me for how I've lived," wept José as he related the drug dealing and gang killing he had been involved in since he was seven years old. José's older brother, Hector, had been a gang member also, but a sidewalk Sunday school had reached him and led him to Christ. Now Hector was reaching out to José, five years younger than Hector.

Hector was responsible for getting his younger brother into the gang in the first place. Now Hector knew that José must get saved. He hung between life and death. José had mixed drugs with alcohol, killings with beatings and immorality with a reckless attitude that led straight to destruction. Thankfully, Hector knew exactly where José was and how to share Christ with him, because Hector had been there once.

At times the best person to share Christ with a lost loved one is one who has walked in his or her steps. When no family member has done that, then that loved one may need to hear the good news from someone who has. For example, a lost family member hooked on drugs or alcohol may need someone who has been there to help him through. It's hard for unsaved people to believe that we as Christians understand their guilt and shame.

You may not be the best person to reach your lost loved ones. Prayer can either bring someone across their paths to reach them or help you identify just the right person to share Christ with them. However, God may use you at times anyway. All of us have had our share of guilt and shame. Being transparent and honest about your guilt can help unsaved family members face theirs.

Hector was the right person to lead José to Christ. Hector understood the guilt and shame José was facing, because he had hit the same wall on his journey to Christ. Let's examine what comprises this wall of guilt and shame and discover some practical ways to help lost loved ones break through the wall and receive Jesus as Lord and Savior.

THE ENEMY'S LIES ABOUT OUR GUILT AND SHAME

For years the enemy has been lying to your lost

family members, which has built a wall of guilt and shame between them and God. Remembering how Satan lied to us helps us share God's truth—the truth that breaks the bondage of guilt and shame. Paul writes:

> If you forgive anyone, I also forgive him. And what I have forgiven—if there was anything to forgive—I have forgiven in the sight of Christ for your sake, in order that Satan might not outwit us. For we are not unaware of his schemes.
>
> —2 CORINTHIANS 2:10–11, NIV

Some people are simply so proud and their hearts so hard that they can't admit or recognize their sin. Others, however, have been so shamed by their past sins that they feel hopelessly trapped in guilt and shame.

One response to guilt and sin is to deny it and cover it over with pride and the wall of self. But another response is to hide the guilt and live in shame. Such was the response of Adam and Eve.

> The woman was convinced. The fruit looked so fresh and delicious, and it would make her so wise! So she ate some of the fruit. She also gave some to her husband, who was with her. Then he ate it, too. At that moment, their eyes were opened, and they suddenly felt shame at their nakedness. So they strung fig leaves together around their hips to cover themselves.

> Toward evening they heard the LORD God
> walking about in the garden, so they hid them-
> selves among the trees.
>
> —GENESIS 3:6–8

Their guilt produced shame, which, in turn, sent them into hiding. Shame makes us vulnerable to the lies of the enemy. What are Satan's lying schemes to keep the lost away from the truth? Here are some of his most common lies that serve as bricks to build a wall of guilt and shame between them and God:

Lie #1: My sins are too terrible to be forgiven by God.

When lost family members believe this lie, they regard themselves as *bad,* while all saved people are *good.* They accept the lie that some sins are much more difficult for God to forgive than others. Furthermore, they wrongly believe that their guilt is particularly horrible and shameful so there is no point in even asking God to forgive such terrible sin.

Jesus dealt directly with this lie when He was brought the woman caught in adultery. As we all know, He asked any who had no sin to cast the first stone at her. Of course, no one did. Even though the self-righteous leaders exposed the shame of this adulterous woman, Jesus didn't condemn her. Instead, He confronted the self-righteous religious leaders.

When family members build the wall of shame and guilt by believing the lie that their shame is too terrible to be forgiven, it's important for you to take these three steps:

1. Be vulnerable, honest, open and transparent.

Before you ask them to confess their sin, confess yours. They need to know that we all have sinned and that none of us is good. All of us need to confess openly that God forgave our sins. There is no sin He cannot or will not forgive. Jesus came to take away the sin of the world (John 1:29). No individual's sins are greater than all the sin of the world, and Jesus forgave it all!

2. Don't be shocked by or judgmental about their sin. Invite your lost family members to share with you the sin or guilt they believe God cannot forgive. Assure them that since God has forgiven you so much, you will certainly be as forgiving, merciful and loving to them as He has been to you. Calmly listen to their confession of sin. Don't interrupt or ask for purulent details. Besides, their confession is to God, not to you.

3. Assure them of God's promise to forgive all sin. Share the following scriptures with your lost loved ones. These are two of many passages that counter the lie of Satan with God's truth.

> But if we confess our sins to him, he is faithful and just to forgive us and to cleanse us from every wrong.
>
> —1 JOHN 1:9

> When we were utterly helpless, Christ came at just the right time and died for us sinners. Now, no one is likely to die for a good person, though someone might be willing to die for a person who is especially good. But God showed his

great love for us by sending Christ to die for us while we were still sinners. And since we have been made right in God's sight by the blood of Christ, he will certainly save us from God's judgment. For since we were restored to friendship with God by the death of his Son while we were still his enemies, we will certainly be delivered from eternal punishment by his life. So now we can rejoice in our wonderful new relationship with God—all because of what our Lord Jesus Christ has done for us in making us friends of God.

—ROMANS 5:6–11

Remember this: God's truth counteracts the lie of the enemy. Always lead a lost loved one back to the truth, not just to your feelings, beliefs or experiences. They need to hear directly from God what He says about their wall of guilt and shame.

Lie #2: No church and no believer will accept me if they find out what I have done.

Your lost family members may wrongly feel that even if God accepts them and forgives their sins, no church will accept them. Our cultural problem is that some churches have been so outspoken against certain sins that nonbelievers feel rejected and condemned.

I visited with a heartbroken father whose two homosexual sons had died. His sons felt so rejected by Christians that they hid their homosexuality from their father for years. Their wall of guilt and shame had been helped along by people in the church who loudly and proudly condemned homosexuals. Both sons believed that even if they accepted Christ as Lord and Savior, the church could never accept them.

Every church should have a sign posted that reads, "We reserve the right to accept anyone here." Paul writes, "So accept each other just as Christ has accepted you; then God will be glorified" (Rom. 15:7). While a holy God never tolerates sin, He lovingly accepts and forgives people while saying, "Go and sin no more."

Can we accept the sinner while not tolerating the sin? Do our family members regard us as likely to reject them if we knew the truth about their past sin and guilt? If so, reach out with God's forgiving love and prove them wrong.

Lie #3: I'm not good enough to be a Christian.

Many lost family members simply feel unworthy to become Christians. They think they must do something to earn God's love and approval. The truth is that God will never love us more than He loves us now. His unconditional love has already given us His Son to die on the cross for our sins. How could He love us any more than that? Still, the unsaved often believe that they are not good enough, that they are unworthy to be saved. Jesus answered this lie with the simple story about a lost sheep.

If you had one hundred sheep, and one of them

strayed away and was lost in the wilderness, wouldn't you leave the ninety-nine others to go and search for the lost one until you found it? And then you would joyfully carry it home on your shoulders. When you arrived, you would call together your friends and neighbors to rejoice with you because your lost sheep was found. In the same way, heaven will be happier over one lost sinner who returns to God than over ninety-nine others who are righteous and haven't strayed away!

—LUKE 15:4–7

Tell your lost family members that they hold more of the Lord's attention than those already "in the fold." God risks everything to redeem the lost!

This raises some tough questions about ourselves. If we spend all our time with the saved, how will we reach the lost? If we want to associate only with good family members, how will the lost black sheep of our families ever hear the Good News? What are we doing to go after the lost in our families? Seeking them out with the Good News of Jesus communicates to them that they are worthy and important to the Lord.

Lie #4: I can never break the habit, addiction or cycle of sin in my life.

The devil seeks to convince us that we are powerless. That seems true because without Christ we are indeed lost, powerless, hopeless and helpless. But the Bible proclaims otherwise.

For nothing is impossible with God.

—LUKE 1:37

For I can do everything with the help of Christ who gives me the strength I need.

—PHILIPPIANS 4:13

If you have a lost family member who feels hopelessly trapped in sin, ask God to break that addiction. Then share about Christ's power with him or her. God's promises to break all bondages and to set us free to live an abundant life are true.

Lie #5: I must change and become a good person before I can get saved.

How often have we tried to make the lost jump through our hoops before they get saved? The enemy uses this lie both in the body of Christ and in the lives of the lost. In the church, the enemy tries to get believers prejudiced against the lost. Religious prejudice demands that people dress, talk, act and behave a certain way. That's religious legalism, not the gospel. Jesus' invitation is simply, "Come."

Remember the story of Zacchaeus, the tax collector? Zacchaeus changed his wicked ways *after* he met Jesus, not *before*.

> There was a man there named Zacchaeus. He was one of the most influential Jews in the Roman tax-collecting business, and he had become very rich. He tried to get a look at

Jesus, but he was too short to see over the crowds. So he ran ahead and climbed a sycamore tree beside the road, so he could watch from there.

When Jesus came by, he looked up at Zacchaeus and called him by name. "Zacchaeus!" he said. "Quick, come down! For I must be a guest in your home today."

Zacchaeus quickly climbed down and took Jesus to his house in great excitement and joy. But the crowds were displeased. "He has gone to be the guest of a notorious sinner," they grumbled.

Meanwhile, Zacchaeus stood there and said to the Lord, "I will give half my wealth to the poor, Lord, and if I have overcharged people on their taxes, I will give them back four times as much!"

Jesus responded, "Salvation has come to this home today, for this man has shown himself to be a son of Abraham."

—LUKE 19:2–9

Jesus invites your lost loved ones simply to follow Him. Following Jesus produces change; change does not produce Jesus. That's the lie of self-actualization, remember? The truth is that we are powerless to change until we accept Christ.

Do we have any unrealistic expectations of our lost family members? Are we putting any religious laws on them or asking them to follow any unwritten rules before they come to church or to Christ? Let's examine ourselves and change our thinking if necessary.

THE DEBT IS TOO GREAT FOR ANYONE TO PAY EXCEPT JESUS!

How do we approach our family members who have built a wall of guilt and shame because of their sin? We approach them with forgiveness. Jesus taught us to pray:"And forgive us our debts, as we forgive our debtors" (Matt. 6:12, NKJV).

The truth is that no one has enough of what it takes to pay off our debt of sin except Jesus, the sinless Lamb of God. The good news for our lost loved ones is that we as believers have no choice but to forgive them of all debts. Furthermore, God has already forgiven them of every sin. Guilt and shame have been erased by the blood of Jesus' sacrifice on the cross.

Tell your lost loved ones that nothing they can do will make Jesus accept them, and that nothing they can do will make Jesus stop loving them.

These two truths shatter the wall of guilt and shame, replacing it with love, forgiveness and acceptance. Will you share these truths with your lost family members and demonstrate through your love the forgiveness, love and mercy of Jesus Christ?

PRAYING FOR YOUR LOST LOVED ONES

When you discern the wall of guilt and shame in your lost loved ones, ask God to give you a heart of mercy, compassion and forgiving love for them. If you expect them to change before coming to Christ, you're only reinforcing the lie of the enemy. If you communicate either verbally or nonverbally that they are unworthy to be saved, you add bricks to their walls. If you do not forgive their sins against you, you perpetuate the enemy's lie that God will not forgive certain sins—and they will have a harder time believeing that God is a forgiving and loving God.

So pray for God's heart of mercy and compassion to fill you.

Lord Jesus, give me Your heart for the lost. Fill me with forgiveness and compassion. Overflow in me such love that I can forgive all my family members of any of their sins against me. Jesus, give me the love You have for the lost. Amen.

Pray this prayer adapted from Lamentations 3:22–33 for your lost loved ones, inserting their names:

The unfailing love of the Lord never ends! By His mercies _____ has been kept from complete destruction. Great is His faithfulness to _____; His mercies begin afresh each day.

I will say, "The Lord is my inheritance; therefore, I will hope in Him for the salvation of _____ !"

The Lord is wonderfully good to those who wait for Him and seek Him. It is good to wait quietly for _____ to be saved by the Lord. And it is good for _____ to submit to the yoke of His discipline.

Let _____ sit alone in silence beneath the Lord's demands. Let _____ lie face down in the dust; then at last there is hope for him/her. Let _____ turn the other cheek to those who strike them. Let _____ accept the insults of his/her enemies.

For the Lord does not abandon _____ forever. Though He brings grief, He also shows compassion according to the greatness of His unfailing love for _____. Amen.

Like the wall of guilt and shame, another wall keeps our loved ones from Jesus—the wall of hurt, anger and bitterness. Let's see how we can discern and dismantle it.

CHAPTER 9

THE WALL OF HURT, ANGER AND BITTERNESS

For years Erin had worked in the church's nursery and toddler class—first as a faithful volunteer and then as a part-time paid attendant. She was loyal and loved children. Then came the fateful run-in with a parent who decided to make life miserable for Erin.

According to the mother, Erin could do nothing right in caring for her toddler. Casey was often crying when her mother came to pick her up. Casey's mother blamed Erin, but the truth was that Casey was quite aggressive with the other kids. Some mornings she had to be restrained so she wouldn't continually hit the other children on their heads. She had quite a punch!

Erin's heart was right with God, and her motives were pure. Nurturing children in God's love was Erin's gifting for ministry in the church. But having a parent always criticize her upset her in a big way! Casey's mother eventually went to their pastor and challenged him to remove Erin from nursery work.

The pastor hated confrontation. Since Erin was gentle and agreeable, the pastor chose the easy way out. To keep peace, he asked Erin to leave the nursery for a while. Instead of confronting the aggressive, hostile parent, he dismissed the gentle, unassuming nursery worker.

For a while, Erin accepted the pastor's unjust action. But her disappointment grew into helpless desperation as she sat in services week after week without a way to serve the Lord with her talents. A number of parents tried to encourage Erin by telling her how much they missed her in the nursery. But their well-meaning remarks only deepened the hurt she felt.

As weeks turned into months, Erin began to skip services. Yet few people called or noticed. She felt that after all those years of faithful service in the nursery she was no longer appreciated, noticed or cared for.

Erin's hurt turned to anger. She was angry with the pastor, with hypocritical Christians and with the church. Months turned into years as Erin allowed bitterness to dominate her feelings about church and God.

Motivated primarily by anger, she pursued a degree

in child development and became the director of one of the most successful and highly respected childcare facilities in the community. Erin succeeded in showing everyone that she was skilled and well-equipped—much more than the church believed, she reasoned. She came to believe that the world showed her more respect and treated her better than Christians did. Hence, she preferred the world's ways to the hurtful ways she had experienced in church.

How sad it is that the church is often an army that shoots its wounded!

THE BRICKS IN THE WALL OF HURT, ANGER AND BITTERNESS

I often talk with former church members who are backslidden. They prayed for healing or for a particular need and were disappointed that God didn't do what they wanted. I have talked with parents who have lost a baby or a child and have been so distraught that they turned their backs on God. People can easily become wounded when expectations are not met.

Do you have family members who are:

- Angry at God?
- Hurt over the way they were treated at church or by Christians?
- Embittered by expecting a miracle that didn't happen in their timing or their way?

Such people can harden their hearts toward God and find many excuses for not receiving Jesus as Lord:

- If that's the way Christians act in business, I want nothing to do with God.
- If that's the way churches are, then forget Christianity.
- I can get hurt by anyone and everyone. Why would I want to go to a church that hurts me, too?
- Other people treat me better than Christians do, so I will go with them.
- All Christians are hypocrites. If Jesus is supposed to change people, and they are not changed, then why follow Jesus?
- I live a better life and act better than most Christians. So why do I need to change?

I could list scores of reasons why people get hurt, become angry and finally grow bitter toward Christians, the church and God. But the truth is, people do get offended and turn their backs on God. It's important to discover the root of the hurt in order to break down the wall.

STEPS TO BREAK THROUGH THE WALL OF HURT

Discover the root of the wound.

Think about the wounded family members you have been praying for and trying to reach with the gospel. What is the root of their hurt?

- ⤺ A Christian hurt them.
- ⤺ They have become disappointed with God.
- ⤺ The church hurt them.
- ⤺ A pastor or leader hurt them.
- ⤺ Other: _____

If you don't know the root of the hurt, anger or bitterness, pray and ask the Holy Spirit to reveal the hurt to you. Then you can begin to break down the wall.

Step #2: Go to the person and repent.

Though you may not have caused the hurt, you can repent for the sins of others. To understand this, let's look at Daniel's prayer for God's people. Though Daniel himself was a righteous and just man, he willingly repented for the sins of his people:

> I prayed to the LORD my God and confessed:"O Lord, you are a great and awesome God! You always fulfill your promises of unfailing love to those who love you and keep your commands. But we have sinned and done wrong. We have rebelled against you and scorned your commands and regulations. We have refused to listen to your servants the prophets, who spoke your messages to our kings and princes and ancestors and to all the people of the land.
>
> "Lord, you are in the right; but our faces are covered with shame, just as you see us now. This is true of us all, including the people of

Judah and Jerusalem and all Israel, scattered near and far, wherever you have driven us because of our disloyalty to you. O Lord, we and our kings, princes, and ancestors are covered with shame because we have sinned against you."

—Daniel 9:4–8

We must be willing as Christians both to pray for repentance and to repent openly and directly to family members who have been hurt by our people—Christians. Wait for the prompting of the Holy Spirit, then go to your wounded family members and repent.

Ask about other wounds.

Ask your family member to share with you any other hurt caused them by the body of Christ. Be open and vulnerable. One way you can witness to your lost family member is to model humility and repentance. Repent of any sin on behalf of the church to your family member.

Tell them who ultimately gets hurt.

Share with your family members the truth that unhealed hurts ultimately hurt only the person who is holding on to them. Encourage them to forgive. If they are disappointed in God, don't defend God. He doesn't need your defense. Simply explain that holding on to anger against God keeps them from receiving His love. Being angry doesn't change God, but it will change them for the worse.

ANGER AGAINST SELF

One type of brick in the wall of hurt, anger and bitterness is anger with oneself. At times people feel that they have so hurt or disappointed themselves or God, that they can never recover from being angry and bitter with themselves.

The only way to approach a person angry with himself is to assure that person of God's unconditional love and unending mercy. The wall of guilt and anger resulting from failure can be immediately dismantled through confession and repentance. To remain angry with one's self in the face of God's forgiveness simply denies His forgiving love and mercy.

John writes, "We will be confident when we stand before the Lord, even if our hearts condemn us. For God is greater than our hearts, and he knows everything" (1 John 3:19–20). God's love is greater than any anger or bitterness against ourselves!

PRAYING FOR YOUR LOST LOVED ONES

Pray in this manner for a lost loved one who is bitterly hurt and angry with God or the church:

> *Lord Jesus, heal the hurt in _____'s heart. Help _____ let go of unresolved anger and replace it with love for You and others. Pull out the root of bitterness and bring _____ to You in repentance. Send Your Spirit to convict _____ that this unhealed hurt, unresolved anger and root*

of bitterness is only destructive and brings no comfort. Amen.

The final wall keeping our lost loved ones from receiving Jesus is the wall of doubt and skepticism. This wall can be overcome through reaching out in prayer and with love.

CHAPTER 10

THE WALL OF
DOUBT AND SKEPTICISM

George had two graduate degrees and an unhealthy abundance of doubt and skepticism about everyone and everybody—including Jesus, Christians and the church. His liberal intellectualism gave him tools for criticizing the historical Bible. George believed the liberal scholarship that demythologized the Bible and gave rational explanations for every miracle and wonder in Scripture.

While in graduate school, George came home during breaks and holidays, loaded with ways to attack his parents' faith in Christ. He chided them for their naïve, immature world-view called Christianity.

Religious faith, George believed, was for the simple-minded and uneducated. His learning freed him from credulous faith and helped him embrace rational, reasoned doubt about anything and anyone—especially God.

George would boastfully make statements like, "I've asked God to prove Himself and do a miracle, and He never has. God never answers my prayers. I've never seen any convincing proof that God exists. The Bible is filled with errors and inconsistencies."

George's parents were at a loss. They didn't know how to counteract George's sophisticated and complex philosophical arguments against the existence of God. And they became weary of George's negative, skeptical attitude toward everything spiritual. In short, they simply gave up trying to talk to him about Jesus so they could have a decent relationship with him.

ARGUING IS NOT THE ANSWER

Because I have a liberal, academic education, I have tried over the years to argue with my intellectual family members about Christ. My intellectual arguments were often more powerful and brilliant than theirs, and I used them to persuade and even browbeat. At times, I won the arguments. But I found out that beating people in a debate does not win them to Jesus. They simply leave determined to be better prepared for the next debate.

The apostle Paul tried to debate a king who was hard of heart:

And as he thus spake for himself, Festus said with a loud voice, Paul, thou art beside thyself; much learning doth make thee mad.

But he said, I am not mad, most noble Festus; but speak forth the words of truth and soberness. For the king knoweth of these things, before whom also I speak freely: for I am persuaded that none of these things are hidden from him; for this thing was not done in a corner. King Agrippa, believest thou the prophets? I know that thou believest.

Then Agrippa said unto Paul, Almost thou persuadest me to be a Christian.

—ACTS 26:24–28, KJV, EMPHASIS ADDED

Even with all his training and education, Paul could not persuade Agrippa to believe. Leading a lost family member to Jesus is not about winning debates or proving who's smarter or better educated. Paul writes that the gospel must be accompanied with God's power to overcome the walls of unbelief in people.

For when we brought you the Good News, it was not only with words but also with power, for the Holy Spirit gave you full assurance that what we said was true. And you know that the way we lived among you was further proof of the truth of our message.

—1 THESSALONIANS 1:5

It is not persuasiveness but the power of God that leads others to Christ.

KEYS TO BREAKING THROUGH THE WALL
OF DOUBT AND SKEPTICISM

The following keys to breaking though the wall of skepticism and doubt will help to unlock the door to your lost family member's heart:

Key #1: Don't debate.

Winning a lost loved one to Jesus doesn't consist of winning a debate, argument or fight. We are not boxers in a ring trying to knock an opponent out. Overpowering an opponent is not the appropriate model. Rather, we are reaching out with the love of Christ. Paul reminds us:

> The Lord's servants must not quarrel but must be kind to everyone. They must be able to teach effectively and be patient with difficult people. They should gently teach those who oppose the truth. Perhaps God will change those people's hearts, and they will believe the truth. Then they will come to their senses and escape from the Devil's trap. For they have been held captive by him to do whatever he wants.
>
> —2 TIMOTHY 2:24–26

We must avoid taking the bait to argue, no matter how tempting or how good a comeback we have. Instead, look for ways to serve that person. Look for ways to demonstrate love and caring. Move the relationship from an intellectual level to a heart level.

There is no debate regarding love.

Key #2: Focus on Jesus.

When sharing Jesus with a skeptical or doubtful person, don't be sidetracked by debates about complex theological issues. Simply point to the core of the gospel:

- Jesus taught us how to live our lives.
- Jesus died for our sins.
- God raised Jesus from the dead.
- Receiving Jesus Christ as Lord and Savior saves us from sin and gives us eternal life.

Share what Jesus has done in your life. No one can debate the impact Jesus has had in you and the change you have experienced. Avoid debating about the church or how other Christians live. Don't split theological hairs about Scripture. Make Jesus the center of your attention and discussion.

Key #3: Ask them what they will do with Jesus.

How we respond to Jesus is the key to salvation. Every person must either accept Him as Lord and Savior, the Son of the living God, or reject Him. There are only two options. The question hasn't changed in two millennia:"What think ye of Christ?" (Matt. 22:42, KJV).

There are only three ways to view Christ: 1) He is who He says He is; 2) He's a liar; or 3) He's deluded and crazy.

When was the last time you asked a loved one who was intellectually skeptical what he or she thought of Jesus?

Key #4: Pray for them.

Prayer is much more effective than debate. When we pray for the lost, we bring to bear in the spiritual realm all the power of God's Spirit to reach them in whatever way possible. Unbelief and skepticism are caused by the enemy to blind your lost loved one to the gospel. "The god of this age has blinded the minds of unbelievers, so that they cannot see the light of the gospel of the glory of Christ, who is the image of God" (2 Cor. 4:4, NIV).

PRAYING FOR YOUR LOST LOVED ONES

At times, we will not even know how to pray. We must simply pray in the power of His Spirit, trusting Him to pray through us, according to Romans 8:26–28:

> *Spirit of God, help me in my weakness. I do not know how I ought to pray, but, Holy Spirit, make intercession for me with groanings that cannot be uttered. Now search my lost loved one's heart and reveal to me the mind of the Spirit for my loved one. Help me to pray and intercede according to Your will. For I know and trust that all things work together for good to those who love God, to those who are called according to His purpose. I believe I am called according to Your will to pray for my lost*

family member so that everything might work together for Your good purpose. In Jesus' name, amen.

So what will overcome the wall of unbelief and skepticism in unbelieving family members? The mind of Christ breaks the bondage of spiritual blindness and gives sight to them. Pray for the mind of Christ to touch the lives of your unbelieving family members and give them eyes to see and ears to hear Jesus.

SECTION III

WILL YOU
PRAY?

⁀

The most effective tool God has given you for winning lost family members to Christ is prayer. As E. M. Bounds said often in his books and messages, "Without prayer you can do nothing."

Prayer helps you know how to share the Scriptures with your family members. Prayer empowers you to understand the walls of separation between you and them. Prayer brings God's will from heaven to earth. Prayer is the key to your family's salvation.

At the beginning of this book I shared with you how Lot led his family into destruction. Instead of being like Lot, we can be like Noah and trust God to build an ark of salvation for our families.

It was by faith that Noah built an ark to save his family from the flood. He obeyed God, who warned him about something that had never happened before. By his faith he condemned the rest of the world and was made right in God's sight.

—Hebrews 11:7

Take a moment to examine your heart and your faith on these three questions:

- Do you trust God to save your family?
- Do you believe that He is able to rescue them from destruction and hell?
- Do you truly accept that God's will for your family is that they be saved?

If you answer a bold, resounding *Yes!* to each of these questions, then it's time to build a prayer ark of salvation for your family. Decide now that nothing in life is more important than the salvation of your family, your children and your children's children. Make a decision now that corresponds to Joshua's decision, "But as for me and my family, we will serve the Lord" (Josh. 24:15).

When Paul and Silas were released from jail by the angel, the Philippian jailer and his whole household were saved. Paul and Silas reassured the jailer:

"Believe on the Lord Jesus and you will be saved, along with your entire household." Then they shared the word of the Lord with him and

all who lived in his household. That same hour
the jailer washed their wounds, and he and
everyone in his household were immediately
baptized. Then he brought them into his house
and set a meal before them. He and his entire
household rejoiced because they all believed
in God.

—Acts 16:31–34

It's time to go after the salvation of your entire
household—not just your immediate family, but every
relative you have!

For years I had prayed for all my relatives to be
saved, whether I knew them or not. Then one evening
I received a long distance phone call from a distant
cousin I never knew I had. This cousin had the same
last name I did and lived in California, while I live in
Florida.

My newfound cousin had been in a Christian bookstore and had seen a book I had written. Having done
research into our family tree, he knew I was a relative
when he saw my name.

This cousin had been saved years ago and boldly
prayed for the salvation of everyone in the family he
knew was still living. How we rejoiced together on the
phone as we met one another as brothers in Christ,
not just cousins in the natural! He and his wife have
since joined us on mission trips and seminars. And
we have joined together in prayer for other unsaved
family members. Together we believe that one day we
will see our entire family saved.

Praying for lost loved ones works! So in this next section we will examine:

- Specific ways to pray for your family
- How to pray for specific family members and their salvation
- How to break bondages that may be holding lost family members captive
- Ways to choose the right words to say at the right time
- How to rely on the guidance of the Holy Spirit

Are you a Noah? Will you be like Joshua? Then pray aloud (in agreement with another believing family member if possible) this covenant prayer adapted from Joshua 24:14–20:

> *I and my family will honor the Lord and serve Him wholeheartedly. We will put away forever the idols our ancestors worshiped. We will serve the Lord alone. As for me and my family, we will serve the Lord. We will never forsake the Lord and worship other gods. For the Lord our God is the one who rescued us and our ancestors from slavery in sin. He performed mighty miracles before our very eyes. As we traveled through the wilderness among our enemies, he preserved us. It was the Lord who drove out and defeated our enemies. So we too will serve the Lord, for He alone is our God. Amen.*

Now let's journey together, praying in faith to build an ark of salvation for our families!

CHAPTER 11

POWER PRAYING
FOR FAMILY SALVATION

For years my brother-in-law Alan had lived a roller-coaster life. At times his relationship with God seemed on track, while at others times he appeared to be completely backslidden and caught up in worldly lusts and passions.

He went through a series of divorces, jobs and cross-country moves. Once during a really rough time of his life, he lived with us for a few months. As a master mechanic, he taught me much about cars. As we worked together tuning up my vehicles, we talked at length about Jesus. Alan always seemed open to Jesus and often confessed his love for and faith in Christ. But his life continued to plunge into dark valleys, and those times looked on the surface like a complete abandonment of Jesus and a total surrender to the world.

The only verse of encouragement my wife and I had for Alan seemed to be Paul's advice, "Accept Christians who are weak in faith, and don't argue with them about what they think is right or wrong" (Rom. 14:1). We refused to argue with Alan about religion.

While he lived with us, we encouraged him to follow Jesus and come with us to worship. Often he went to the altar to weep and pray. But once he left our home, he returned to worldly ways.

My wife (Alan's sister) and I prayed and waited on God for Alan. Alan's parents, who adopted him as a toddler, prayed unceasingly for him through all the trials and valleys. They never gave up. They always supported his efforts to return to the Lord after living as a prodigal. For over forty years they prayed and waited on God for Alan's salvation.

Alan's last wife, Shay, converted to Christ after their divorce. God put a supernatural love in her heart for Alan even though he had treated her badly and left her. After her conversion Shay became an aggressive, bold witness for Christ in Alan's life. She wrote, called and met with Alan often to share about Jesus. Years after their divorce, she maintained contact and continued to pray for him, hoping that one day Alan would repent and return home to the Lord—perhaps even to her.

Prayers of agreement are perhaps the most powerful prayers we can pray. Jesus said, "I also tell you this: If two of you agree down here on earth concerning anything you ask, my Father in heaven will do it for you. For where two or three gather together because they are mine, I am there among them" (Matt. 18:19–20). Four believers were agreeing together continually for Alan's salvation—his ex-wife, his sister and both parents.

One evening out of the blue, Alan called Shay. She hadn't talked with him for weeks. Apparently he had hit bottom. Rejected by his latest girlfriend and out of a job, Alan found himself lost, alone and feeling totally abandoned. He wept tears of broken repentance as he confessed his situation to Shay, expressing his desire to come home both to God and to her.

Shay immediately left in her van to drive across the country to pick up Alan and bring him home. They met in Phoenix and began a drive back to the East Coast. On the second day of their trek, after having talked much about the Lord, they decided to stop at a famous roadside chapel to recommit their lives to Christ and to reaffirm their marriage vows. Alan surrendered himself to Jesus in that chapel.

Just hours later on the interstate highway headed east, the axle of their van broke, sending them and their van tumbling side over side in the median. Alan was killed at the scene of the accident while Shay spent weeks in intensive care recovering from her injuries.

At Alan's memorial service, our pastor read an inspiring and moving passage from Isaiah:

> The righteous pass away; the godly often die
> before their time. And no one seems to care or
> wonder why. No one seems to understand that
> God is protecting them from the evil to come.
> For the godly who die will rest in peace.
>
> —ISAIAH 57:1–2

Knowing Alan's history of struggling with the world's temptations, we believed that God had gracefully spared Alan, *protecting him from the evil to come.* Though his death seemed untimely, we know now that God's grace reached out to him in a supernatural way.

PRINCIPLES OF POWER PRAYING

Prayer isn't passive—it's active, effective and powerful! James asserts:

> Are any among you sick? They should call for
> the elders of the church and have them pray
> over them, anointing them with oil in the name
> of the Lord. And their prayer offered in faith will
> heal the sick, and the Lord will make them well.
> And anyone who has committed sins will be
> forgiven. Confess your sins to each other and
> pray for each other so that you may be healed.
> The earnest prayer of a righteous person has
> *great power and wonderful results.*
>
> —JAMES 5:14–16, EMPHASIS ADDED

Prayer warrior Dick Eastman of Every Home for Christ writes:

Evelyn Christenson, in her guide *Evangelism Prayer,* not only provides a sound biblical case for praying for our neighbors, but suggests many of our evangelism efforts might be unfruitful because we do not properly employ two spiritual weapons. Those weapons are the authority of the name of Jesus (John 16:24) and the authority of the blood of Jesus (Ephesians 1:17; Revelation 12:1). I would add another weapon to the list: the authority of the Word of God (Ephesians 6:17; Revelation 12:11). This involves the tactical use of the Scriptures in our spiritual warfare.[1]

Let's see how to apply these aspects of power praying. I suggest first finding someone to pray in agreement with. When we gather in His name with another believer (a spouse, family member or friend), power is increased.

PRAYING IN THE AUTHORITY
OF THE NAME OF JESUS

Praying in the name of Jesus ushers in His presence. When the Lord is present, miracles happen because nothing is impossible. Jesus promises:

> Where two or three come together in my name, there am I with them.
>
> —MATTHEW 18:20, NIV

155

> When you are assembled in the name of our Lord Jesus and I am with you in spirit, and the power of our Lord Jesus is present...
>
> —1 CORINTHIANS 5:4, NIV

Jesus promises that praying in His name will bring an answer to our prayers:

> And whatever you ask in My name, that I will do, that the Father may be glorified in the Son.
>
> —JOHN 14:13, NKJV

> You did not choose me, but I chose you and appointed you to go and bear fruit—fruit that will last. Then the Father will give you whatever you ask in my name.
>
> —JOHN 15:16, NIV

> Until now you have not asked for anything in my name. Ask and you will receive, and your joy will be complete. Though I have been speaking figuratively, a time is coming when I will no longer use this kind of language but will tell you plainly about my Father. In that day you will ask in my name.
>
> —JOHN 16:24–26, NIV

The name of Jesus is exalted above every name, and all authority is in Him. That means everything in heaven and earth must bow before His mighty name (Phil. 2:9–10). So pray this way for your lost loved ones:

*In the name of Jesus, I rebuke you, devil, and all
the demons of hell. Take your hands off
_____. In Jesus' name, I tell you to leave
_____ alone. Blindness, oppression and darkness flee from _____'s life in Jesus' name.*

*Jesus, I ask You to send Your Holy Spirit in every
way through every person who _____ meets
so that he/she will hear about You and believe in
Your mighty name for salvation. Amen.*

All that the name of Jesus contains

When we pray in the authority of the name of
Jesus, we bring to bear all that His name contains for
our lost loved ones. Let's look at the fullness of His
name.

The bread of life (John 6:35). In Jesus' name is both
physical and spiritual provision. Pray in agreement:

*Lord Jesus, You are the bread of life for _____.
You are the source of _____'s every need. By
Your Spirit, convict _____ of his/her absolute
need of You and dependence on You. Amen.*

Living water (John 7:37–38). In Jesus' name is
renewing, refreshing and cleansing. Pray in agreement:

*Lord Jesus, You are living water for _____. You
are the only way that _____ will be cleansed,
renewed and refreshed. As water is necessary for
physical life, so Your living water of the Spirit is
essential for _____'s spiritual life. Flood,*

immerse, baptize and overflow _____ with
Your living water. Amen.

The light of the world (John 8:12). In Jesus' name is insight, wisdom and power over darkness. Pray in agreement:

Lord Jesus, You are the light of the world. Shine your light on _____ . Dispel all darkness from _____'s life. Remove _____'s blindness and fill him/her with the light of Your wisdom, understanding and knowledge so that _____ may become a child of light. Amen.

I AM (John 8:58). Jesus calls Himself the eternal name of God: Yahweh, "I AM WHO I AM" (Exod. 3:14, NKJV). In Jesus' name abides all life and eternity. Pray in agreement:

Lord Jesus, I pray that by the Holy Spirit, You lead _____ into the way of salvation and give _____ the gift of eternal life. Only You, Jesus, have salvation. Only You, Jesus, have the gift of eternal life. I pray that You will be the great I AM for _____. Amen.

The door (John 10:7). Jesus' name is the door to all possibility and newness for the future. He is the door to the ark of salvation we are building by faith in prayer for our families. Jesus also stands at the door of each heart asking to come in: "Look! Here I stand at the door and knock. If you hear me calling and open the door, I will come in, and we will share a meal as friends" (Rev. 3:20). Pray in agreement:

> *Lord Jesus, You are the door of salvation for*
> _____ . *By Your Spirit lead* _____ *through*
> *the door. Invite* _____ *to enter into Your*
> *kingdom. Keep knocking at the door of*
> _____*'s heart. Amen.*

The Good Shepherd (John 10:11). As the Good Shepherd, Jesus nurtures, guides, cares for and protects. Pray in agreement:

> *Lord Jesus, be* _____*'s Good Shepherd. Care*
> *for, nurture, guide and protect* _____ *from the*
> *attack of the enemy who comes to kill, steal and*
> *destroy. Reveal to* _____ *the abundance of life*
> *in You. Amen.*

The resurrection and the life (John 11:25). Through His name, Jesus delivers us from death into life. Jesus has all resurrection power. Pray in agreement:

> *Lord Jesus, I pray for You to raise*_____ *from*
> *his/her death in sin to new life in You. Bring*
> _____ *to the revelation that You alone are the*
> *resurrection and the life. Amen.*

The way, the truth, and the life (John 14:6). By the power of His name, Jesus makes a way where there is no way. He helps us to discern right from wrong, lies from the truth. In Him is life, not just existence and mere survival. Pray in agreement:

> *Lord Jesus, be the way, the truth and the life for*

_____. Guide _____'s life. Take _____ *from merely surviving to living for You. Amen.*

The true vine (John 15:1). In Jesus' name, we are connected and rooted to God. Through His name, our lives produce lasting fruit. Pray in agreement:

Lord Jesus, be the source and true vine for _____. Produce Your fruit in _____'s life when he/she comes to a saving knowledge of You. Amen.

THE BLOOD OF JESUS

The blood of Jesus saves and cleanses us from all sin.

But our High Priest offered himself to God as one sacrifice for sins, good for all time. Then he sat down at the place of highest honor at God's right hand....And so, dear friends, we can boldly enter heaven's Most Holy Place because of the blood of Jesus...For our evil consciences have been sprinkled with Christ's blood to make us clean, and our bodies have been washed with pure water.
—HEBREWS 10:12, 19, 22

As we pray in His name, we apply the blood of Jesus to our family members, asking Jesus to convict, save, heal and deliver them through the power of His blood. Pray in agreement:

I know, Lord Jesus, that by Your stripes and shed

*blood all healing and salvation flows. So I pray
that You reveal the power of Your blood to
_____ so that _____ will be cleansed,
saved, delivered and set free from sin and death.
Amen.*

THE WORD OF JESUS

Jesus revealed to His disciples, "It is the Spirit who gives eternal life. Human effort accomplishes nothing. And the very words I have spoken to you are spirit and life" (John 6:63). Jesus is the Word, and He has the words of life. So we must pray the authority of His Word over the lives of our unsaved family. Try beginning in the Gospels and then move into the rest of the New and Old Testaments, particularly the Psalms.

My daughter Amy's first Bible was given to her by her godly, believing grandmother. In the margin next to John 3:16 her grandmother wrote, "For God so loved AMY, that He gave His only begotten Son, so that if AMY believeth on him, AMY should not perish but have everlasting life."

That word prayed and spoken over Amy had a profound impact on her life. One day while reading her Bible, Amy discovered her special verse. She ran to me as a young child and excitedly said, "Daddy! Daddy! My name is written right here in the Bible."

One Sunday morning a few years later, Amy was in children's church. She asked to leave to come and sit in the sanctuary at the end of the worship service. As the pastor, that day I gave an invitation to receive Christ, and my bubbly, red-headed sweetheart was the first one to come bouncing down the center aisle. She had received into her heart the word that was written and prayed over her years before. Praise the Lord! Today she still lives a sold-out life to Jesus Christ, and so does her spouse and their children. In fact, so do our other two children and their families. God is so faithful and good!

Now, let's look at some tools that will help us pray powerfully for our lost loved ones.

CHAPTER 12

TOOLS FOR
POWER PRAYING

T hough every believer is instructed to pray, I have found that different prayer tools work for different believers. Because of that, I am offering you three prayer tools to get you started power praying for your family. Use whichever fits you the best. Or, take parts of all three of them and create your own power-praying machine! Whatever you do—pray!

TOOL #1: THE FOUR WS

Dick Eastman writes about power praying that watches, walks, wars and wins.[1] Each of these power prayer tools will strengthen your prayer of agreement for family salvation.

Watching. Jesus commanded us to both "watch and pray" (Matt. 26:41, KJV). Paul reaffirmed this when he said, "Devote yourselves to prayer, being watchful" (Col. 4:2, NIV).

Often in the Old Testament, references are made to watchmen on the walls who spy any enemy who might be approaching. Are you watching out for your lost loved ones daily in prayer? Our watching and praying can prevent attacks on them from the enemy.

Walking. God promised Joshua, "I will give you every place where you set your foot" (Josh. 1:3, NIV). Pray as you walk through your home or the home of a lost loved one. Walk over the territory and possess it in Jesus' name. Determine to take back territory that the enemy has stolen.

Surround your lost family members with territory that you have walked and claimed for Jesus. Walk their neighborhoods, workplaces and recreational places, and claim that land and all its inhabitants for the kingdom of God.

Warring. Spiritual warfare involves putting on the whole armor of God and praying all the time with all types of prayers for all the saints (Eph. 6). By faith claim the salvation of your family, calling what is not as though it were. Call them "believers" even though you don't see it yet.

As you war, pull down strongholds and vain imaginations.

We are human, but we don't wage war with human plans and methods. We use God's mighty weapons, not mere worldly weapons, to knock down the Devil's strongholds. With these weapons we break down every proud argument that keeps people from knowing God. With these weapons we conquer their rebellious ideas, and we teach them to obey Christ.

—2 CORINTHIANS 10:3–5

Go to spiritual war and knock down the devil's strongholds of lies, deception, pride, human reasoning, confusion and ignorance.

Winning. We have the power to win. We can overcome anything that hinders us from seeing the full salvation of our household. We must overcome our own walls, the walls of our lost family members and the attacks of the enemy. The victory has already been secured, but we must apply God's Word and promises with the blood of the Lamb to overcome. Scripture reveals:

It has happened at last—the salvation and power and kingdom of our God, and the authority of his Christ! For the Accuser has been thrown down to earth—the one who accused our brothers and sisters before our God day and night. And they have defeated him because of the blood of the Lamb and because of their testimony. And they were not afraid to die.

—REVELATION 12:10–11

Pray boldly in agreement with other believers, knowing that you are a victor, a conqueror and an overcomer in the name of Jesus. Don't quit until you see victory in the life of every family member. Victory over sin. Victory over death and hell. The victory that claims eternal life in Christ Jesus.

> How we thank God, who gives us victory over sin and death through Jesus Christ our Lord! So, my dear brothers and sisters, be strong and steady, always enthusiastic about the Lord's work, for you know that nothing you do for the Lord is ever useless.
> —1 Corinthians 15:57–58

Tool #2: The Seven Positions of Power Praying for Family Salvation

There are at least seven positions of prayer in Scripture. Each position reveals something of the attitude of the one who is praying.

Sitting in prayer. Sitting is resting in the Lord's presence. "For he raised us from the dead along with Christ, and we are seated with him in the heavenly realms—all because we are one with Christ Jesus" (Eph. 2:6). Seated with Christ, you can talk with Him and communicate to Him your concerns. Pray this, inserting your loved one's name:

> *Lord, as I sit with You in heavenly places and rest in Your presence, I seek Your lovingkindness to be*

extended to _____ . *I pray that in Your perfect timing* _____ *will also be seated with You in heavenly places. O Lord, save* _____ *in Jesus' name. Amen.*

Pray for the salvation of your family when you are seated for a meal, driving a vehicle, in a waiting room, at a worship service, at work or in your home.

Kneeling in prayer. Kneeling is a position of submission. As you submit yourself to Jesus, you are asking Him from the position of a servant to save your family. "As Jesus was saying this, the leader of a synagogue came and knelt down before him. 'My daughter has just died,' he said, 'but you can bring her back to life again if you just come and lay your hand upon her'" (Matt. 9:18). Pray:

Lord Jesus, I kneel before You, humbly repenting of any attitude or wall within me that might be keeping my family from salvation. I ask You to save _____ *so that his/her knee might also bow to You as Lord. Amen.*

Take time to pray as you kneel at your bedside, at your desk, in worship, at the altar or in a prayer meeting.

Bowing in prayer. When you bow in prayer, you give honor to the King of kings and Lord of lords. "For this reason I bow my knees to the Father of our Lord Jesus Christ" (Eph. 3:14, NKJV). Honor the Lord for His great mercy and compassion. For your lost family members, you might bow and pray:

Lord Jesus, I honor and adore You for saving me. I honor You for providing the way of salvation for _____. I eagerly look forward to the day when, as one of the family of God, _____ will honor You. Amen.

Standing in prayer. As you stand in prayer, you indicate a readiness and preparedness to do whatever is needed by the Lord. "And when ye stand praying, forgive, if ye have ought against any: that your Father also which is in heaven may forgive you your trespasses" (Mark 11:25, KJV). For lost loved ones, stand and pray:

Lord Jesus, I stand before You seeking what You desire of me. However You need me to witness to and serve _____, I am ready to do so. Your servant stands willingly before You to obey and serve. Amen.

Lying prostrate in prayer. Lying prostrate before God indicates a position of repentance and seeking God for His leading and guidance. "He went on a little farther and fell face down on the ground, praying, 'My Father! If it is possible, let this cup of suffering be taken away from me. Yet I want your will, not mine'" (Matt. 26:39). Pray for the lost:

Lord Jesus, I prostrate myself before Your throne. I beseech You to save _____. I repent of anything I have done to keep _____ from knowing You as Lord and Savior. Forgive me, I pray. Amen.

Lifting hands in prayer. When you pray for the lost, lift up your hands to praise Jesus for His wonderful gift of salvation and to receive all that He has for you. He wants to inhabit your praise. "So wherever you assemble, I want men to pray with holy hands lifted up to God, free from anger and controversy" (1 Tim. 2:8). He desires to fill you with every good gift to reach the lost. Pray with uplifted hands for your lost family members:

> *Lord Jesus, I give You praise for Your gift of salva-tion. I give You praise for all the ways _____ will be touched by the Holy Spirit. I give You praise for the day when all my household is saved. In Jesus' name, amen.*

Laying on hands in prayer. Years ago when our children were infants, Judi and I (separately and together) would go into our children's rooms as they slept and lay hands on them. We prayed both for their salvation and blessing for their future. "So after more fasting and prayer, the men laid their hands on them and sent them on their way" (Acts 13:3).

In Scripture, the laying on of hands imparted blessing, the presence of God's Spirit, anointing, healing and releasing or ordination into ministry. If you have an infant, lay hands on your baby often in prayer for his or her future salvation and blessing. As your child grows, continue to pray for him or her, laying on your hands to impart your blessing and favor. Your children will enjoy hearing your blessing being prayed over them.

Also lay hands on your spouse, relatives and other family members as they give you permission to pray over them for salvation, healing, impartation and blessing. For salvation, you might pray:

Lord Jesus, as I lay my hands on _____, *I ask You to save, heal, deliver and bless* _____. *May he/she always know that You alone, Jesus, are the source of every good thing in life and eternity. Amen.*

THE ACTS OF POWER
PRAYING FOR YOUR FAMILY'S SALVATION

For years I have taught the ACTS of prayer in youth and discipleship training sessions. This acronym can be an excellent guide in praying for your family members.

A—Adoration. "To adore" means "to worship, magnify, bless and glorify the Lord according to His character and nature." During your quiet time, as you drive, sit in a waiting room or have an extra moment at work, pray adoration sentence prayers such as these, inserting your loved one's name:

Jesus, I adore You for Your goodness and mercy in saving me and in giving me the faith to believe for the salvation of _____. *Amen.*

Jesus, I worship Your majesty and give You honor for saving me. I honor You now for the future salvation of _____. *Amen.*

I bless Your name, O Lord, and believe that some day soon _____ will also be blessing Your name when _____ is saved by Your grace. Amen.

For the sake of Your glory, O Lord, save _____. Amen.

C—Confession. "To confess" means in the Greek to "say the same as" or "agree" with another person. When we confess something to Christ, we agree with Him about that issue. When we confess a sin, that means we are agreeing with Him that it is sin. We also confess or declare that He is Lord and Savior. So pray:

Jesus, I confess and pray that _____ will confess that You alone are Lord and Savior of all humanity. Amen.

Jesus, I agree with Your perfect will for the salvation of _____. Amen.

Jesus, I confess that both _____ and I are sinners in eternal need of Your saving grace. Amen.

Jesus, I agree with You that I have both strengths and weaknesses that You can and will use in the salvation of _____. Amen.

T—Thanksgiving. To give thanks requires us to recognize that we did not earn what we have. Thanksgiving means that Jesus is both the source of all we have and the owner—we are simply stewards of His bountiful possessions. So pray:

Jesus, I thank You for my salvation, health, prosperity and blessings. I thank You now for that moment when You will save, heal, prosper and bless _____. Amen.

Jesus, I thank You for the life of _____. I pray that You will reach out with Your strong arm of salvation to save _____. Amen.

Lord Jesus, I am so grateful for everything You have done, are doing and will do for Your name's sake. I am particularly grateful that You died on the cross for _____, and I am eternally grateful that all that can be done in time and eternity for _____'s salvation is being done by Your grace. Amen.

S—Supplication. Supplication is prayer that asks for something either by petition or intercession. We ask humbly and according to God's will, petitioning Him patiently and persistently, not just for our own needs but also for the needs of others.

When we intercede, we want to pray what God desires. As the Spirit prays through us as Paul talks about in Romans 8, we know how to pray for the lost. So pray:

I ask You, Lord Jesus, to save _____. Amen.

I ask You, Lord Jesus, to reveal to me by Your Spirit how to intercede for the salvation of _____. Amen.

Go through the ACTS of prayer for your lost loved

ones regularly. Believe that God will do everything through you and beyond you to reach your lost loved ones with the saving message of Jesus Christ.

Power praying continues patiently in hope and faith. Power praying pulls down the walls within us and breaks down the walls that keep our unsaved families members away from Jesus. Power praying trusts God to do what we cannot do to reach the lost. Power praying surrenders body, soul and spirit to the leading of the Holy Spirit in reaching the lost. Power praying shatters the gates of hell and loosens the enemy's grasp on our loved ones. Power praying confidently knows that "the Spirit who lives in you is greater than the spirit who lives in the world" (1 John 4:4). Start power praying now for the salvation of all your lost family members!

CHAPTER 13

PRAYING GOD'S
WORD FOR
FAMILY SALVATION

W hen we stand in agreement with the Word of God while speaking, praying and confessing it for our families, God's will in heaven is brought to earth. Remember, Jesus defeated the attack of Satan in the wilderness by speaking God's Word. He countered each attack with, "It is written…" (Matt. 4:4, 7, 10, NKJV).

I have discovered that little is more powerful than prayers for family salvation based on the Word of God. That's why this chapter is filled with them. Do you wish your loved ones would get saved? Then pray the Word of God over them. Choose those prayers that specifically apply to your family situations. Praying and claiming God's Word brings life to your family. "He sent His word and healed them, and delivered them from their destructions" (Ps. 107:20, NKJV).

God's healing Word saves, heals and delivers from every destruction and pit in life. The Word of God shatters every wall, breaks every chain, delivers from every bondage and exposes every sin. As you pray and speak His Word over your family, you impart truth and life to them.

Read each verse aloud, then pray the following intercession on behalf of your lost family members. In some instances, I have directly adapted the verse as a prayer for you to pray. Put your lost family member's name in the blanks.

Praying the Image of God Over
Lost Family Members

Then God said, "Let us make people in our image, to be like ourselves. They will be masters over all life—the fish in the sea, the birds in the sky, and all the livestock, wild animals, and small animals."

So God created people in his own image;
God patterned them after himself;
male and female he created them.

—GENESIS 1:26–27

Creator of the universe, You purposed and destined

_____ *to be formed in Your image, which has
been shattered by _____'s sin. Father, send
forth Your Spirit to reveal to _____ that he/she
has been created in Your image and is purposed to
live eternally with You. Draw _____ to Yourself,
bless _____ and save _____, I pray. Amen.*

PRAYING THE BLESSING OF GOD OVER
YOUR LOST LOVED ONES

*Lord, bless _____ and protect _____.
  Lord, smile on _____ and be gracious to
_____.

  Lord, show _____ Your favor and give
_____ Your peace.*
—ADAPTED FROM NUMBERS 6:24–26

PRAYING FOR YOUR CHILD'S SALVATION

We are commanded to instruct our children in the
ways of God:

These are all the commands, laws, and regula-
tions that the LORD your God told me to teach
you so you may obey them in the land you are
about to enter and occupy, and so you and your
children and grandchildren might fear the LORD
your God as long as you live. If you obey all his
laws and commands, you will enjoy a long life.
Listen closely, Israel, to everything I say. Be

careful to obey. Then all will go well with you, and you will have many children in the land flowing with milk and honey, just as the LORD, the God of your ancestors, promised you.

Hear, O Israel! The LORD is our God, the LORD alone. And you must love the LORD your God with all your heart, all your soul, and all your strength. And you must commit yourselves wholeheartedly to these commands I am giving you today. Repeat them again and again to your children. Talk about them when you are at home and when you are away on a journey, when you are lying down and when you are getting up again. Tie them to your hands as a reminder, and wear them on your forehead. Write them on the doorposts of your house and on your gates.

—DEUTERONOMY 6:1–9

Teach me, O Lord, to instruct _____ to love You with all his/her heart, mind, soul and strength. Lord, I commit myself wholeheartedly to obeying Your commands in my home and to repeating them to _____ when he/she lies down, when he/she gets up, when he/she comes in and when he/she goes out. Thank You, Lord, for _____'s salvation. Amen.

PRAYING FOR YOUR HUSBAND'S SALVATION

Lord, grant that _____ does not follow the advice of the wicked, or stand around with sin-

ners, or join in with scoffers. But _____ delights in doing everything You want; day and night he thinks about Your law.

I pray for _____ to be like a tree planted along the riverbank, bearing fruit each season without fail. May his leaves never wither, and in all he does, may my husband prosper. May he repent of the ways of the wicked, for they are like worthless chaff, scattered by the wind. They will be condemned at the time of judgment. Sinners will have no place among the godly.

O Lord, watch over the path of _____. Save my husband, for I know that the path of the wicked leads to destruction. Amen.

—ADAPTED FROM PSALM 1

PRAYING FOR YOUR WIFE'S SALVATION

I praise You, Lord, with my whole heart for my wife, _____. I praise Your holy name. I praise You, Lord, and I will never forget the good wife You have given me.

Forgive, I pray, all of _____'s sins and heal all her diseases. Ransom her from death and surround her with love and tender mercies. Fill my wife's life with good things. Renew her strength like the eagle's!

I praise You, Lord, for that day when my wife is saved! Amen.

—ADAPTED FROM PSALM 103:1–5

PRAYING FOR YOUR PARENT'S SALVATION

Honor your father and mother. Then you will live a long, full life in the land the LORD your God will give you.

—EXODUS 20:12

Lord, I honor _____ by praying for him/her and sharing the Good News of Jesus Christ with him/her. Lord, I thank You for my father/mother. Even as he/she has blessed me with natural life, even more, I desire that he/she be blessed with eternal life through my Savior, Jesus. Lord, save my mom/dad for Your name's sake that I may honor him/her, not just for time, but also for eternity. Amen.

PRAYING FOR YOUR GRANDPARENTS' SALVATION

But the godly will flourish like palm trees
   and grow strong like the cedars of Lebanon.
For they are transplanted into the LORD's own
   house.
They flourish in the courts of our God.
Even in old age they will still produce fruit;
   they will remain vital and green.
They will declare, "The LORD is just!
He is my rock!
There is nothing but goodness in him!"

—PSALM 92:12–15

Lord Jesus, I desire that my grandparents become godly by knowing You in their old age. Turn them from selfishness to surrendering self to You. Plant them like palm trees and transplant them into the house of the Lord. May they hunger and thirst after You, Jesus, in their old age. May they flourish in Your presence!

Father, let the fruit of my grandparents' old age be the joy of salvation and a love for other lost family members. Use my grandparents to declare, "The Lord is just! He is my Rock! There is nothing but goodness in Him!"

PRAYING FOR YOUR GRANDCHILD'S SALVATION

The children of your people
    will live in security.
Their children's children
    will thrive in your presence.
                  —PSALM 102:28

Lord Jesus, I belong to You. Since I am Yours, I claim the promise that _____ will also live in security. I am claiming not only physical and emotional security for _____, but eternal security as well, in the name of Jesus. I boldly stand on Your promise, Lord, that my children's children will thrive in your presence. Amen.

PRAYING FOR YOUR BROTHER'S SALVATION

How wonderful it is, how pleasant,
  when brothers live together in harmony!
For harmony is as precious as the fragrant
    anointing oil
  that was poured over Aaron's head,
  that ran down his beard and onto the border
    of his robe.
Harmony is as refreshing as the dew from
    Mount Hermon
  that falls on the mountains of Zion.
And the LORD has pronounced his blessing,
  even life forevermore.

—PSALM 133

Lord Jesus, how wonderful it is when I am in harmony with my brother, _____. I know that the only way for me to be in complete harmony and unity with him is for both of us to be saved— members of Your family. How precious harmony is to You, O Lord. How refreshing harmony is to Your people. So Lord, pronounce Your blessing on _____ and lead him into the ways of life forevermore. Amen.

PRAYING FOR YOUR SISTER'S SALVATION

O LORD, do not stay away!

You are my strength; come quickly to my aid!
Rescue me from a violent death;
   spare my precious life from these dogs.
Snatch me from the lions' jaws,
   and from the horns of these wild oxen.
Then I will declare the wonder of your name to
   my brothers and sisters.
I will praise you among all your people.
                 —PSALM 22:19–22

Lord Jesus, You are my strength. You have aided me when every enemy has attacked. You have rescued me from violent death. Fill me with praise that I might declare the wonder of Your name to my sister, _____. I will praise You in her presence. I will tell her of Your wonderful salvation and of Your love for both her and me. Amen.

PRAYING FOR THE SALVATION OF
YOUR ENTIRE HOUSEHOLD

Crispus, the leader of the synagogue, and all his household believed in the Lord. Many others in Corinth also became believers and were baptized.
                 —ACTS 18:8

Lord, make me a leader like Crispus so that I may lead my entire family to You. Make me a leader like Noah, leading my whole household into the ark of salvation. Make me a leader like Abram, leading my family out of a sinful land and into Your land of promise. Yes, Lord, make me a leader like Moses, forsaking Egypt for the promised land of Your salvation.

Lord, destroy every wall in me that keeps them from hearing about You through me. Overcome every wall in them so they can receive Your Good News. Lord, I pray for the day when my entire household believes in Your name and is baptized. Amen.

PRAYING THE SINNER'S PRAYER WITH A FAMILY MEMBER

When family members are ready to accept Jesus Christ as Lord and Savior, it will be exciting for you to lead them in prayer. You might follow these steps:

1. Ask them if they wish to accept Jesus Christ as their personal Lord and Savior.
2. When they respond positively, invite them to look at these scriptures with you just to confirm their understanding of the gospel. In fact, it may be better if you have memorized these passages and can share them in your own words: John 3:16; Romans 3:23; Romans 5:6–8; Romans 10:9–11; Ephesians 2:8–9.
3. Invite them to pray a prayer like this with you:

Lord Jesus, I believe that You are the Christ, the

Son of the living God, and I want to receive
You as my personal Lord and Savior. I repent
of my sins and ask Your forgiveness. Thank
You for forgiving my sins through Your death
on the cross. I receive Your forgiveness and
surrender my life completely to You. Thank You
for eternal life and the gift of Your Holy Spirit.
Thank You for saving me. Amen.

4. Encourage your newly saved family members to become involved immediately in a church or small group of believers where they can worship and be discipled.

Now, to make praying for your loved ones simpler, I've included a Forty-Day Prayer Journal. In the entries for the last twenty days are many more scripture prayers that you can use to intercede for all of your lost family members. Pray the Word over every lost family member, because His Word is Spirit and life to them.

SECTION IV

FORTY DAYS OF PRAYER: GETTING YOUR FAMILY SAVED

P rayer is God's ordained way of bringing His kingdom on earth. Throughout the Scriptures, a period of forty days represented a focused time to pray, overcome temptation and seek God.

Job discovered the secret of praying for others: "And the LORD turned the captivity of Job, when he prayed for his friends: also the LORD gave Job twice as much as he had before" (Job 42:10, KJV). During these forty days, you will receive blessing after blessing while praying for the salvation of your family. And that includes the most important blessing of all—seeing lost family members get saved!

During these forty days, you will be tempted to give

up. *What's the use? She'll never get saved. He's a lost cause.* This temptation comes directly from hell. Satan knows that prayer is your most powerful weapon for defeating his schemes to keep family members enslaved to sin. Don't yield to the temptation to quit during these forty days. Keep praying!

FASTING AND PRAYER

You may feel led to fast as you pray. I encourage you to fast and pray as the Spirit leads you. Fasting is not essential, but if God leads you to fast—do so!

First, claim Jesus' promise concerning fasting:

> And when you fast, don't make it obvious, as the hypocrites do, who try to look pale and disheveled so people will admire them for their fasting. I assure you, that is the only reward they will ever get. But when you fast, comb your hair and wash your face. Then no one will suspect you are fasting, except your Father, who knows what you do in secret. And your Father, who knows all secrets, will reward you.
>
> —MATTHEW 6:16–18

What reward are you seeking? A treasure in heaven—and the salvation of your loved ones is one of the greatest rewards of all.

Consider the fast of Nineveh. Fearing God's destruction, the people fasted until God's wrath was averted and the city was saved.

The people of Nineveh believed God's message, and from the greatest to the least, they decided to go without food and wear sackcloth to show their sorrow. When the king of Nineveh heard what Jonah was saying, he stepped down from his throne and took off his royal robes. He dressed himself in sackcloth and sat on a heap of ashes. Then the king and his nobles sent this decree throughout the city: "No one, not even the animals, may eat or drink anything at all. Everyone is required to wear sackcloth and pray earnestly to God. Everyone must turn from their evil ways and stop all their violence. Who can tell? Perhaps even yet God will have pity on us and hold back his fierce anger from destroying us."

When God saw that they had put a stop to their evil ways, he had mercy on them and didn't carry out the destruction he had threatened.

—JONAH 3:5–10

When applying this story to praying for the salvation of our families, we can infer that prayer and fasting touches the heart of God's mercy for the lost.

DIVISIONS OF THE PRAYER JOURNAL

During the first twenty days of prayer, you will be reaching out to touch the heart of God as you also reach out to share His love with your lost family members. Each day will include:

- A *promise* of salvation from the Word of God. Consider memorizing these verses.
- A brief *meditation* on that scripture to encourage you.
- An *action step with prayer* you can take to reach out to your lost family members with God's love.

During the second twenty days of prayer, you will be praying and confessing the Word over your lost family members. Each day will include a scripture adapted just for praying over them.

I want to encourage you to pray these scriptures over your lost family members again and again. Pray them until you have them memorized. Pray them until they are deposited in your heart and etched in your thoughts. Then you can use the sword of the Spirit to attack spiritual strongholds and walls both in your life and theirs any time and anywhere you want.

I encourage you not only to go through these forty days now for a family member, but to go through this journal again and again for each lost family member until all are saved!

I am agreeing with you in prayer by faith for the salvation of your whole household. Amen!

A FORTY-DAY
PRAYER JOURNAL

DAY 1
PRAY IN AGREEMENT

Promise: Read Matthew 18:19–20

Meditation

God's will is that the lost be saved. When you agree with another believer in faith according to God's will, He acts to keep His promise. You can trust God's Word!

If you are married and your spouse is a believer, pray with your mate. Two people who are one in Christ form the strongest bond that exists for praying in agreement. Don't let up. Never quit. Continue to agree in prayer for the salvation of your children, your children's children, your parents, your siblings and other relatives. Pray for their salvation—it is God's will!

Action Step With Prayer

Find a prayer partner. Arrange specific and regular times to pray together. Write a prayer of agreement for the salvation of your lost loved ones, and pray it together.

DAY 2
PRAY IN HIS NAME

Promise: Read John 15:16

Meditation

The most important fruit your life can bear are people saved from hell to live eternally with Christ. What kind of fruit is your life bearing?

You are God's chosen vessel to witness to Him first in Jerusalem, then in Judea, Samaria and around the world. (See Acts 1.) Your Jerusalem is that place closest to you—your home, your family and your close relationships. Asking in His name is asking in His will, for His way, in His timing and for His glory. Are you asking for the salvation of your lost family?

Action Step With Prayer

Decide today that you will persist in prayer for your lost loved ones until all are saved. Write a prayer asking God for the fruit of saved souls in your life, including the salvation of your lost loved ones.

_____

_____

_____

_____

_____

_____

DAY 3
APPLY THE BLOOD OF JESUS

Promise: Read Hebrews 9:11–12

Meditation

You can boldly enter the throne room of the King of kings and the Lord of lords. Boldly approach God to seek the salvation of your family. You have nothing to fear. By His blood you have been given access to the holy of holies. Ask what you desire in His will, and it will happen.

Do you fervently desire that your family have access to the throne of Christ as you do? Then apply the blood of Jesus over your family for protection and healing. Ask Jesus to send His Spirit to reveal the power of His shed blood on the cross to all your lost family.

Action Step With Prayer

Draw a cross. On that cross write down the names of the loved ones for whom you are praying. Write a prayer of thanks for the blood Jesus shed for your family.

Day 4
Tear Down the Wall of Prayerlessness

Promise: Read Psalm 77:1–4

Meditation

Are you too distressed to pray? Then trade your sorrow for something that really makes a difference— prayer. Your prayers will move heaven and earth in Jesus' name.

It's time to stop worrying over your lost family members. Instead pray now for each lost family member by name. Pray with the hope and expectation that each will be saved.

Action Step With Prayer

Write the names of your unsaved family members on an index card. Keep it in your purse or wallet as a daily reminder to pray for their salvation. Write a prayer asking God to remove the wall of prayerlessness from your life as you pray daily for your lost loved ones.

_____

_____

_____

_____

_____

DAY 5
OVERCOME APATHY

Promise: Read Luke 15:8–10

Meditation

Are you filled with zeal and enthusiasm for winning your lost family to Christ? If you lost something valuable, you would turn everything upside down to find it, right? Your lost family members are much more valuable than any lost possession.

Apathy will cause you to stop praying, cease hoping and give up witnessing. Apathy hardens your heart to how important and valuable every single soul is to God. Just one sinner repenting invokes choruses of joy in heaven. Keep seeking your lost family members until each one has prompted a joyful symphony in heaven!

Action Step With Prayer

Write the names of your lost family members with an erasable marker on your bathroom mirror so that every morning you will pray for their salvation. Write a prayer asking God to fill you with zeal and enthusiasm as you share Jesus with your lost family members.

Day 6
Tear Down the Wall of Condemnation

Promise: Read Romans 8:1–2

Meditation

We are not under condemnation, therefore we don't need to condemn others. Jesus' sacrifice on the cross—not anything we have done—has freed us from condemnation.

His sacrifice is also offered freely to all the lost people on the planet. They must choose whether they want freedom or whether they prefer to stay under the bondage of sin. What Jesus has done to set you free is good news to all your lost family members. Are you treating them with the same love that Jesus has for them? Have you told them about the wonderful freedom from condemnation that you've experienced in Christ Jesus? If not, when will you?

Action Step With Prayer

Find a way to show affirmation and appreciation for your lost family members. Write a prayer asking God to fill you with His love and acceptance so that you don't condemn your lost loved ones.

_____

_____

_____

_____

DAY 7
TEAR DOWN THE WALL OF WORLDLY LIVING

Promise: Read Ephesians 2:2–7

Meditation

Stop living as the world lives! Your life may be the only Bible your lost loved ones will ever read.

You are a living letter from God to them. Your example will have a great impact on how they respond to the love of God in Christ Jesus. God's favor and mercy will be best seen in your actions. Decide today to set aside worldly ways for God's ways so that all that your family sees in you is Jesus.

Action Step With Prayer

Examine your life. Write a prayer asking God to remove any worldly way from your life.

_____

_____

_____

_____

_____

_____

DAY 8
TEAR DOWN THE WALL OF UNBELIEF

Promise: Read Matthew 13:58

Meditation

Let me ask you a pointed question. Do you really believe that God can and will save your lost family members? Or is your unbelief keeping you from seeing the miracle of salvation in their lives?

No lost person is beyond the reach of God's saving love. God is profoundly concerned with each person's salvation even when you are not. So dedicate yourself right now to trust and believe in God's miracle-working power of salvation.

Action Step With Prayer

Write a prayer listing all the reasons you trust God to save your family members. Pray this prayer aloud daily as a confession of your faith in His saving power.

_____

_____

_____

_____

_____

_____

DAY 9
TEAR DOWN THE WALL OF FEAR

Promise: Read 2 Timothy 1:7

Meditation

In sharing Jesus with your lost family members, what do you fear most?

❑ Rejection
❑ Sounding stupid, ignorant or superspiritual
❑ Ridicule
❑ Not knowing all the answers to all their questions
❑ Other _____

God has given you the power to be a witness and to be used as a vessel of power, signs and wonders. God has filled you with love and empowered you to love others. And He gives you self-control and a sound mind so that no one—and I mean no one—can intimidate you. So, you have nothing to fear!

Action Step With Prayer

Decide how you will share Jesus with one of your family members. Then write a prayer asking God to remove fear from your life and give you the power to share with your family member.

_____

_____

_____

Day 10
Tear Down the Wall of Arrogance

Promise: Read Ephesians 4:2

Meditation

You are not spiritually superior to the lost. Knowing how great God's mercy is to us as sinners should humble us and destroy every ounce of pride in us. Your humility and gentleness will go much further in winning your lost family members to Christ than any knowledge you have of Scripture or any piety you demonstrate.

Be patient with your lost family members. Do not expect them to understand spiritual language or spiritual ideas that took you years to understand. Your job is not to impress your lost family with your spiritual maturity but rather to impress them with Jesus.

Action Step With Prayer

Repent immediately whenever you realize you are being proud or rude with others. Write a prayer asking the Lord to make you meek and humble, convicting you when you are proud or rude.

_____

_____

_____

_____

_____

Day 11
Tear Down the Wall of Busyness

Promise: Read Matthew 22:2–5

Meditation

When the King summons you to an important event, are you too busy? The King has summoned and commissioned you and me to go into all the world and make disciples. He has commanded us to be His witnesses beginning in Jerusalem (at home) and going into all the world.

Are you too busy to heed His command? Are you too busy to reach out to your lost loved ones? What keeps you so busy—chores, work, recreation, the television, household tasks? What will it take for you to make time to obey the King's commands?

Action Step With Prayer

Take one busy but nonessential task you have to do today and replace it with a more important task—praying for or witnessing to a lost family member. Write a prayer asking the Lord to forgive you for being too busy.

_____

_____

_____

_____

_____

Day 12: Tear Down
the Wall of Love Growing Cold

Promise: Read Matthew 24:12–14

Meditation

Love seeks. Love refuses to be passive and complacent. We can become so comfortable with the lost state of some of our family members that we are lulled into complacency. That's exactly what the enemy wants. When we accept the lost state of unbelievers and tolerate the fact that they are destined for hell, then our love has grown cold for them.

True love means loving others the way God loves us. We love because He first loved us and gave Himself for us (1 John 4). How are you showing your Christ-like love to your unsaved family members? Will you love them the way God loves you?

Action Step With Prayer

Jot down three ways you can show God's love this month to your lost loved ones. Write a prayer of thankfulness for God's love for you and your lost loved ones.

_____

_____

_____

_____

_____

Day 13
Believe God for Boldness

Promise: Read Acts 4:31

Meditation

God is your sure defense. You have nothing to fear with your unsaved family members. They cannot harm or hurt you. God will protect you and guide you in all your ways.

That means you can be bold. The truth is on your side. Boldness is not brashness, but it is confidence. Boldness is not rude, but it often does intrude. Boldness is never unkind, but it does speak the truth in love. Boldness knows that the most loving thing you can do for your family is to lead them to Jesus.

Action Step With Prayer

Write a prayer asking God to fill you with boldness and give you the right words to say to your lost loved ones.

_____

_____

_____

_____

_____

DAY 14
REPENT AND TRUST JESUS

Promise: Read Acts 2:38–39

Meditation

When we repent and trust Jesus, we not only receive eternal life, but we also receive an eternal promise—the promise of salvation and eternal life in Christ Jesus for us and for our children. They can come to a saving knowledge of Jesus just as we did.

Are you believing for your children to come to Christ? Are you trusting Jesus not only to save them, but also to give them the gift of the Holy Spirit?

Action Step With Prayer

Tell your children today about an answer to prayer that you received. Write a prayer of thanksgiving to God for the promise of eternal life and salvation of your children.

DAY 15
ADMIT FALLING SHORT

Promise: Read Romans 3:23

Meditation

It's important to live a transparent, open and true life with others. They need to know how good God is—and that we are not God. Being saved doesn't make us perfect. Our lost family members need to know how we struggle, fail and sin at times, but that Jesus never gives up on us.

How difficult is it for you to admit your mistakes to your lost family members? Will you let them see how much you need Jesus? Being saved is not about being good; it's about being His. The lost can learn about the mercy and forgiveness of God by hearing you admit your mistakes and failures.

Action Step With Prayer

Write a prayer asking the Lord to teach you to be transparent and honest about your sins, mistakes and failures. The next time you fail at something around a lost family member, admit it, quit it and forget it.

DAY 16
KNOW GOD LOVES YOU

Promise: Read Romans 5:6–11

Meditation

When you were helpless, Christ died for you. Now your lost family members are helpless. Christ has also died for them. Even if they are God's enemies, you cannot treat them as your enemies. Besides, we are commanded to love our enemies. So how are you showing God's love to your lost loved ones?

The only way your lost family members can know that God loves them is if you tell them and show them. Telling is not enough. Loving words are empty without loving actions. Find ways to show His love to them.

Action Step With Prayer

Write a prayer asking God to show you a practical way to show His love to a lost family member. Then do it this week.

_____

_____

_____

_____

_____

Day 17
Believe and Confess

Promise: Read Romans 10:9–11

Meditation

When we believe with our hearts, our feelings and affections are fixed on Jesus. We love Him passionately. He is the source of our joy and peace. As we believe in our hearts that God raised Him from the dead, resurrection life wells up within us and flows out of us like living water.

What we confess with our mouths is what comes out of our hearts. What is in your heart? The confessing of your mouth announces God's next victory in your life. What are you believing? What are you speaking?

Action Step With Prayer

Write a prayer confessing that Jesus is the Son of God and claiming the salvation of your family.

DAY 18
CALL ON THE NAME OF THE LORD

Promise: Read Romans 10:13

Meditation

How will your lost family members hear of the name of Jesus? How will they know the wonderful promise of salvation? They need to hear about Jesus from you.

Often, the only time our lost loved ones hear the name of Jesus is when it is spoken in a curse. They will not know that His name means "God saves" unless you share with them who He is. The promise of salvation is for anyone and everyone. Let them know how important they are to Jesus!

Action Step With Prayer

Before the name of Jesus ever reaches your lips, examine your heart. Be certain that His name is only spoken as a blessing and not in any derogatory fashion. Write a prayer asking forgiveness for using the Lord's name in foolish and profane ways.

_____

_____

_____

_____

_____

DAY 19
KEEP TELLING THEM

Promise: Read Romans 10:14–15

Meditation

Too often we depend on others to tell our lost family members about Jesus. We take them to church, hoping the preacher will tell them. We drag them to a conference or seminar, hoping that the speaker will convince them. We seek out people at church with an evangelistic spirit to speak to them, hoping they will reach our family. But still not much happens.

Don't become discouraged. Keep telling them about Jesus yourself. No matter how many other people may cross paths with your loved ones speaking Jesus' name, you tell them about Him as well. You lay up treasures for yourself in heaven each time you honor the name of Jesus and share the gospel.

Action Step With Prayer

Decide now that the next time you talk with a family member, you will find a way to talk about Jesus. Write a prayer asking God to make you aware of every opportunity for sharing the gospel.

DAY 20
CLAIM THE PROMISE OF GOD'S LOVE

Promise: Read John 3:16–17

Meditation

Jesus came into the world to save you and your family. God's love gave His Son to us to die on the cross for our sins. There is no greater love!

When you talk about love with your lost family members, talk about the love of God. Tell them often that you love them and God loves them. Also share with your lost family members that you are praying for God's love to touch and save them.

Action Step With Prayer

How will you tell your lost loved ones today about the Father's love? Find a way...make a way...and then do it.

_____

_____

_____

_____

_____

_____

Day 21
Pray for Bondages to Be Broken

*The Spirit of the Sovereign Lord is upon me,
because the Lord has appointed me to bring good
news to* _____. *He has sent me to comfort*
_____ *when* _____ *is brokenhearted and
to announce that he/she can be released and set
free.*

He has sent me to tell _____ *that the time
of the Lord's favor has come, and with it, the day of
God's anger against every enemy. When* _____
*is sad, the Lord will give beauty for ashes, joy
instead of mourning, praise instead of despair.*

I am believing for You, Lord, to plant _____
*like strong and graceful oak, for Your own glory.
Amen.*

—ADAPTED FROM ISAIAH 61:1–3

Write down how God is answering your prayers
today:

_____

_____

_____

_____

_____

_____

DAY 22
PRAY AGAINST THE DARKNESS

By faith in Jesus I confess that in the beginning the Word already existed. He was with God, and He was God. He was in the beginning with God. He created everything there is. Nothing exists that He didn't make.

Life itself was in Him, and this life gives light to everyone, including _____. The light shines through the darkness in his/her life, and the darkness can never extinguish it.

I know that You, Lord, have sent me to tell _____ about the light so that everyone might believe because of my testimony.

You, Jesus, are the true light, who gives light to _____, although he/she does not yet recognize You as Savior and Lord.

But to everyone in my family who believes in and accepts Him, You will give the right to become children of God. They will be reborn—not with a physical birth resulting from human passion or plan, but reborn from God. Amen.

—ADAPTED FROM JOHN 1:1–13

Write down how God is answering your prayers today:

_____

_____

_____

Day 23
War Against the Enemy

I confess that as I put on all of God's armor I will be able to stand firm against all strategies and tricks of the devil. I am not fighting against my family, but against the evil rulers and authorities of the unseen world.

I will use every piece of God's armor to resist the enemy in the time of evil.

I will stand my ground, believing for the salvation of _____, putting on the sturdy belt of truth and the body armor of God's righteousness. For shoes, I put on the peace that comes from the Good News, so that I will be fully prepared. In every battle I will need the faith of God as my shield to stop the fiery arrows aimed at me and at _____ by Satan. I put on salvation as a helmet and take up the sword of the Spirit, which is the Word of God. Lord, help me to pray at all times and on every occasion in the power of the Holy Spirit. Help me stay alert and be persistent in my prayers for all my family. Amen.

—Adapted from Ephesians 6:10–18

Write down how God is answering your prayers today:

_____

_____

_____

DAY 24
PULL DOWN STRONGHOLDS

Lord, I seek to use Your mighty weapons, not merely worldly weapons, to knock down the devil's strongholds. With these weapons, Lord, I know that I will break down every proud argument that keeps _____ from knowing You. With these weapons I will conquer his/her rebellious ideas and teach _____ to obey Jesus Christ. Amen.

—ADAPTED FROM 2 CORINTHIANS 10:4–5

Write down how God is answering your prayers today:

Day 25: Pray the Word of My Testimony and the Blood of the Lamb

I rejoice in the salvation and power and kingdom of our God, and the authority of His Christ!

I declare according to Your Word that the accuser has been thrown down to earth—the one who accused our brothers and sisters before our God day and night.

I know that the enemy is defeated because of the blood of the Lamb and because of my testimony that Jesus Christ is Savior and Lord.

So, devil, take your hands off my family in the name and by the blood of Jesus. Amen.

—Adapted from Revelation 12:10–11

Write down how God is answering your prayers today:

_____

_____

_____

_____

_____

_____

_____

_____

DAY 26
PRAY IN THE POWER OF THE SPIRIT

Jesus, help me continue to build the lives of my family on the foundation of Your holy faith. Holy Spirit, direct me in how to pray for my family.

Empower me to live in such a way that God's love can bless ＿＿＿＿＿ and me as we wait for the eternal life that our Lord Jesus Christ in His mercy is going to give us.

Help me show mercy to those whose faith is wavering.

O Lord, rescue ＿＿＿＿＿ by snatching him/her from the flames of judgment. There are still others to whom I need to show mercy, but keep me safe from their sin.

And now, all glory to You, God, who is able to keep ＿＿＿＿＿ from stumbling, and who will bring ＿＿＿＿＿ into Your glorious presence, innocent of sin and with great joy.

All glory to You, God, who alone is God our Savior. Yes, glory, majesty, power and authority belong to You—in the beginning, now and forevermore. Amen.

—ADAPTED FROM JUDE 20–25

Write down how God is answering your prayers today:

＿＿＿＿＿＿＿＿＿＿＿＿＿＿＿＿＿＿＿＿＿＿＿

＿＿＿＿＿＿＿＿＿＿＿＿＿＿＿＿＿＿＿＿＿＿＿

＿＿＿＿＿＿＿＿＿＿＿＿＿＿＿＿＿＿＿＿＿＿＿

Day 27
Release Anger

Lord Jesus, renew my thoughts and attitudes. Display through me a new nature because I am a new creation, created in God's likeness— righteous, holy and true.

Help me, Lord, put away all falsehood and tell my family the truth because we belong to each other. Jesus, empower me to overcome sin so that anger will have no control over me. Convict me so I will not let the sun go down while I am still angry, for I know that anger gives a mighty foothold to the devil.

Inspire me to give generously to others in need, especially those in my family who need the saving knowledge of Jesus Christ.

Keep me from using foul or abusive language. Let everything I say be good and helpful, so that my words will be an encouragement to everyone in my family, including those who are lost.

Keep me from grieving Your Holy Spirit by the way I live. I remember that He is the one who has identified my family and me as His own, who will be saved on the day of redemption. Amen.

—Adapted from Ephesians 4:23–30

Write down how God is answering your prayers today:

_____

_____

Day 28
Release Guilt

*Our Father in heaven, may Your name be honored
in _____'s life. May Your kingdom come soon
in _____'s life. May Your will be done in
_____'s life, just as it is in heaven.*

Give _____ food for today.

*Forgive his/her sins, just as I have forgiven
_____, who has sinned against me.*

*And don't let _____ yield to temptation, but
deliver _____ from the evil one.*

*Let Your kingdom, power and glory be mani-
fested in _____ when _____ receives Your
Son as Lord and Savior. Amen.*

—Adapted from Matthew 6:9–13

Write down how God is answering your prayers
today:

_____

_____

_____

_____

_____

_____

_____

DAY 29
RELEASE UNBELIEF

*Lord, I believe that You can and will save
_____. I ask You to rescue _____ from the
one who rules in the kingdom of darkness, and to
bring _____ into the kingdom of Your dear
Son. For You, God, have purchased _____'s
freedom with Jesus' blood and have forgiven all
_____'s sins.*

*Christ, I confess that You are the visible image
of the invisible God. You existed before God made
anything at all, and You are supreme over all creation.*

*For you, Christ, are the one through whom God
created everything in heaven and earth. You made
the things we can see and the things we can't
see—kings, kingdoms, rulers and authorities.
Everything has been created through You and for
You.*

*You existed before everything else began, and
You hold everything in creation together, including
_____. Amen.*

—ADAPTED FROM COLOSSIANS 1:13–17

Write down how God is answering your prayers
today:

_____

_____

_____

Day 30
Release Religious Bondages

*Lord Jesus, shatter every religious bondage in
_____ with Your love. Reveal to _____
that Your love is patient and kind, not envying or
boastful.*

Shatter _____'s pride with Your love.

*Overcome _____'s rudeness and self-
seeking with Your lovingkindness and mercy.*

*Lord, help _____ understand that Your
loving mercy keeps no record of wrong but
always rejoices in right.*

*With Your love, protect _____ until he/she
comes to a saving knowledge of You. Amen.*

—Adapted from 1 Corinthians 13:4–7

Write down how God is answering your prayers
today:

_____

_____

_____

_____

_____

_____

_____

Day 31
Adore God for Salvation

Jesus, give me the courage, love and boldness to pass on to _____ the truth and good news that You died for our sins, just as the Scriptures say.

You were buried, and You were raised from the dead on the third day, as the Scriptures say.

You were seen by Peter and then by the twelve apostles. After that, You were seen by more than five hundred of Your followers at one time. Then You were seen by James and later by all the apostles.

O Jesus, give me now such a beautiful vision of You that my joy of salvation will enthrall, captivate and lead all my family to You. Amen.

—ADAPTED FROM 1 CORINTHIANS 15:3–8

Write down how God is answering your prayers today:

_____

_____

_____

_____

_____

DAY 32
GLORIFY GOD FOR HIS GRACE

I long for all my family to enter the courts of the Lord. With my whole being, body and soul, I shout joyfully to You, the living God. O Lord Almighty, my King and my God, how happy is the family who can live in Your house, always singing Your praises. Happy is the family who is strong in the Lord. When they walk through the Valley of Weeping, it will become a place of refreshing springs, where pools of blessing collect after the rains! They will continue to grow stronger, and each of them will appear before God. O Lord God Almighty, a single day in Your courts is better than a thousand anywhere else! I would rather my family be gatekeepers in the house of my God than live the good life in the homes of the wicked. No good thing will the Lord withhold from those who do what is right. O Lord Almighty, happy is the family who trusts in You. Amen.

—ADAPTED FROM PSALM 84

Write down how God is answering your prayers today:

_____

_____

_____

_____

DAY 33
THANK GOD FOR HIS BLESSINGS

I shout with joy to the Lord! I worship the Lord with gladness. I come before Him, singing with joy.

I acknowledge that the Lord is God! He made my family, and we are His. We are His people, the sheep of His pasture.

I pray for that day when my whole family will enter His gates with thanksgiving and go into His courts with praise. I give thanks to Him and bless His name.

For the Lord is good. His unfailing love to my family continues forever, and His faithfulness to save, heal and deliver my family continues to each generation. Amen.

—ADAPTED FROM PSALM 100

Write down how God is answering your prayers today:

_____

_____

_____

_____

_____

DAY 34
PRAY TO GOD FOR HIS MERCY

*Jesus, my eyes are always looking to You for help,
to You alone, Lord Jesus, to rescue _____ from
the traps of _____'s enemies.*

*Turn to _____ and have mercy on him/her,
for _____ is alone and in deep distress.
_____'s problems go from bad to worse. Oh,
save _____ from them all! Feel _____'s
pain and see _____'s trouble. Forgive all
_____'s sins. See how many enemies
_____ has, and how viciously they hate
him/her! Protect _____! Rescue _____'s
life from them!*

*I pray that the day will soon come when
_____ puts all his/her trust in You! Amen.*

—ADAPTED FROM PSALM 25:15–21

Write down how God is answering your prayers
today:

_____

_____

_____

_____

_____

_____

DAY 35
BE CRUCIFIED WITH CHRIST

*O Jesus, I desire above all to be crucified with You
so that I no longer live, but You live in me.*

*I desire that the life I now live, I will live by
trusting You completely.*

O Jesus, You loved me and gave Yourself for me.

*Help me to die to self so that _____ might
see Your saving love in me and be saved! Amen.*

—ADAPTED FROM GALATIANS 2:19–20

Write down how God is answering your prayers today:

_____

_____

_____

_____

_____

_____

_____

_____

_____

Day 36: Believe for the Salvation of My Immediate Family

Lord, You have tested my thoughts and examined my heart in the night. You have scrutinized me and found nothing amiss, for I am determined not to sin in what I say.

I have followed Your commands, which have kept me from going along with cruel and evil people. My steps have stayed on Your path; I have not wavered from following You.

I am praying to You because I know You will answer, O God. Bend down and listen as I pray.

Show _____ Your unfailing love in wonderful ways. Save _____ with Your strength as _____ seeks refuge from the enemy.

Guard _____ as the apple of Your eye. Hide _____ in the shadow of your wings. Amen.

—Adapted from Psalm 17:3–8

Write down how God is answering your prayers today:

_____

_____

_____

_____

_____

_____

Day 37
Praise the Lord for My Family

The Lord remembers us, and He will surely bless us. He will bless those of my family who serve Him.

He will bless those who fear the Lord, both great and small.

May the Lord richly bless both me and my children. May my family be blessed by the Lord, who made heaven and earth.

The heavens belong to the Lord, but He has given the earth to all humanity.

The dead cannot sing praises to the Lord, for they have gone into the silence of the grave. But my family can praise the Lord both now and forever! Praise the Lord! Amen.

—Adapted from Psalm 115:12–18

Write down how God is answering your prayers today:

_____

_____

_____

_____

_____

_____

_____

Day 38
Look Forward to That Day

*I know, Lord, that You are not slow about Your
promise to return, as some people think. I know
that You do not want anyone to perish, so You are
giving more time for _____ to repent.*

*But the day of the Lord will come as unexpect-
edly as a thief. Then the heavens will pass away
with a terrible noise, and everything in them will
disappear in fire, and the earth and everything on
it will be exposed to judgment. Since everything
around us is going to melt away, what a holy,
godly life I desire to live!*

*I look forward to that day and hurry it along—
the day when God will set the heavens on fire and
the elements will melt away in the flames. I am
looking forward to the new heavens and new earth
You have promised, a world where all my family,
including _____, is right with God. Amen.*

—Adapted from 2 Peter 3:9–13

Write down how God is answering your prayers
today:

_____

_____

_____

_____

_____

Day 39
Rejoice in the Lord's Return

Almighty God, I believe that Jesus died and was raised to life again.

I also believe that when Jesus comes, God will bring back with Him all the Christians, and I am praying for all my family to be included.

For the Lord Himself will come down from heaven with a commanding shout, with the call of the archangel, and with the trumpet call of God. First, all the Christians who have died will rise from their graves.

Then, together with them, we who are still alive and remain on the earth will be caught up in the clouds to meet the Lord in the air and remain with Him forever.

I am comforted and encouraged as I believe You for the salvation of all my family so that together we may rejoice on the day of Your return. Amen.

—ADAPTED FROM 1 THESSALONIANS 4:14–18

Write down how God is answering your prayers today:

_____

_____

_____

_____

Day 40
Rejoice in Eternal Life With Jesus

Write down all the answers to prayers you have seen in the last forty days:

_____

_____

_____

_____

Write down the names of all the members of your family who are saved:

_____

_____

_____

_____

Write a prayer of thanksgiving for their salvation:

_____

_____

_____

_____

Write down the names of your family members you are believing to be saved in Christ:

_____

_____

_____

_____

Write a prayer of thanksgiving for the gift of salvation Jesus has offered each member of your family, and praise Him for that day when all your household will be saved!

_____

_____

_____

_____

CONCLUSION

My Prayer for You

I ask the Lord to protect you,

Put you under the shadow of His wing,

Encourage you never to quit,

Give you the right words to say,

Remove every wall in you and in your family that hinders a saving relationship with Jesus

And draw you near to Him.

I pray that the Lord Jesus will fill you with the Holy Spirit and give you the power to continue praying for all your family members, with all kinds of prayers, all the time, until all are saved! In Jesus' mighty name, amen.

NOTES

CHAPTER 1: THE WALL OF WORLDLY LIVING

1. Michael Brown, *Go and Sin No More* (Ventura, CA: Regal Books, 1999), 264.

CHAPTER 2: THE WALL OF PRAYERLESSNESS

1. Jack W. Hayford, *Prayer Is Invading the Impossible* (South Plainfield, NJ: Logos International, 1977; rev. ed., Bridge Publishing, 1995), 92.
2. Peter C. Wagner, Confronting the Powers (Ventura, CA: Regal Books, 1996), 242.

CHAPTER 3: THE WALL OF CONDEMNATION

1. Robert S. McGee, *The Search for Significance* (Nashville, TN: Word Publishing, 1988), 59

CHAPTER 6: THE WALLS OF RELIGIOUS ARROGANCE, BUSYNESS AND LOVE GROWING COLD

1. Ted Haggard, "A Pinch of Kindness and Humility," *Ministries Today*, January/February 2000, p 25.

CHAPTER 7: THE WALL OF SELF

1. Keith Miller, *Sin: Overcoming the Ultimate Deadly Addiction* (San Francisco, CA: Harper and Row Publishers, 1987), 66–67.

CHAPTER 11: POWER PRAYING FOR FAMILY SALVATION

1. Dick Eastman, *Watching, Walking, Warring—And Winning: The Lighthouse Movement Handbook* (Sisters, OR: Multnomah Publishers, 1999), 27.

CHAPTER 12: TOOLS FOR POWER PRAYING

1. Eastman, Watching, *Walking, Warring—And Winning: The Lighthouse Movement Handbook*, 25–28.

Dr. Larry and Judi Keefauver reside outside of Orlando, Florida. Their ministry, YMCS (Your Ministry Counseling Services), conducts seminars and workshops equipping believers to pray for family members, grow spiritually in marriage and communicate effectively in families.

You may contact their ministry for more information or prayer:

Dr. Larry Keefauver
YMCS & The Gathering Place
P.O. Box 950956
Lake Mary, FL 32795
1-800-950-5306
1-407-324-5006 (fax)
lkeefauv@bellsouth.net

Other books by Dr. Larry Keefauver with Creation House include:

Lord, I Wish My Husband Would Pray With Me
Lord, I Wish My Family Would Get Saved
Praying With Smith Wigglesworth
Healing Words
Smith Wigglesworth on Prayer
Smith Wigglesworth on Healing
Smith Wigglesworth on Faith
The Azusa Street Devotional
The John G. Lake Devotional
The Maria Woodworth-Etter Devotional
The Smith Wigglesworth Devotional

Dr. Keefauver is the general editor of *The Holy Spirit Encounter Bible* and eight Holy Spirit Encounter Guides (Creation House).

Other books by Dr. Keefauver are:

Hugs for Grandparents
When God Doesn't Heal Now
Friend to Friend (with J. David Stone)
Friends and Faith

You can experience more of *God's grace & love!*

If you would like free information on how you can know God more deeply and experience His grace, love and power more fully in your life, simply write or e-mail us. We'll be delighted to send you information that will be a blessing to you.

To check out other titles from **Creation House** that will impact your life, be sure to visit your local Christian bookstore, or call this toll-free number:

1-800-599-5750

For free information from Creation House:

CREATION HOUSE
600 Rinehart Rd.
Lake Mary, FL 32746
www.creationhouse.com

Your Walk With God Can Be Even Deeper...

With *Charisma* magazine, you'll be informed and inspired by the features and stories about what the Holy Spirit is doing in the lives of believers today.

Each issue:
- Brings you exclusive world-wide reports to rejoice over.
- Keeps you informed on the latest news from a Christian perspective.
- Includes miracle-filled testimonies to build your faith.
- Gives you access to relevant teaching and exhortation from the most respected Christian leaders of our day.

Call 1-800-829-3346 for 3 FREE trial issues
Offer #AOACHB

If you like what you see, then pay the invoice of $22.97 (**saving over 51% off the cover price**) and receive 9 more issues (12 in all). Otherwise, write "cancel" on the invoice, return it, and owe nothing.

Experience the Power of Spirit-Led Living